PRISM

READING AND WRITING 4

Jessica Williams

with
Wendy Asplin
Christina Cavage

CAMBRIDGE
UNIVERSITY PRESS

Shaftesbury Road, Cambridge CB2 8EA, United Kingdom

One Liberty Plaza, 20th Floor, New York, NY 10006, USA

477 Williamstown Road, Port Melbourne, VIC 3207, Australia

314–321, 3rd Floor, Plot 3, Splendor Forum, Jasola District Centre, New Delhi – 110025, India

103 Penang Road, #05–06/07, Visioncrest Commercial, Singapore 238467

Torre de los Parques, Colonia Tlacoquemécatl del Valle, Mexico City CP 03200, Mexico

Cambridge University Press & Assessment is a department of the University of Cambridge.

We share the University's mission to contribute to society through the pursuit of
education, learning and research at the highest international levels of excellence.

www.cambridge.org
Information on this title: www.cambridge.org/9781009251990

First published 2017
Update published 2022

20 19 18 17 16 15 14 13 12 11 10 9 8 7 6 5 4 3 2 1

Printed in Mexico by Litográfica Ingramex, S.A. de C.V.

A catalogue record for this publication is available from the British Library

ISBN 978-1-009-25199-0 Student's Book with Digital Pack 4 Reading and Writing
ISBN 978-1-316-62544-6 Teacher's Manual 4 Reading and Writing

CONTENTS

SCOPE AND SEQUENCE

UNIT	WATCH AND LISTEN	READINGS	READING SKILLS	LANGUAGE DEVELOPMENT	
1 CONSERVATION *Academic Disciplines* Architecture / Information Technology / Urban Planning	Preserving CDs at the Library of Congress	1: Are We Living in the Digital Dark Ages? (article) 2: To the County Board regarding Cook County Hospital (letters)	*Key Skills* Identifying an argument Identifying supporting details *Additional Skills* Using your knowledge Previewing Understanding key vocabulary Reading for main ideas Reading for details Making inferences Skimming Identifying purpose Synthesizing	Time expressions Compound adjectives	
2 DESIGN *Academic Disciplines* Graphic Design / Marketing	The Role of Helvetica Font in Graphic Design	1: What Makes a Successful Logo? (textbook chapter) 2: Rebranding and Logos (textbook chapter)	*Key Skills* Taking notes in outline form Making inferences *Additional Skills* Previewing Understanding key vocabulary Reading for main ideas Reading for details Identifying purpose Predicting content using visuals Making inferences Synthesizing	Describing emotional responses Paraphrasing	
3 PRIVACY *Academic Disciplines* Business / Law Enforcement / Media	Computer Fraud: Celebrity Hacking	1: Cyber Harassment (article) 2: Combatting Cyber Harassment (essay)	*Key Skill* Identifying purpose and tone *Additional Skills* Understanding key vocabulary Using your knowledge Previewing Reading for details Reading for main ideas Identifying purpose and tone Synthesizing	Collocations for behavior Problem-solution collocations	
4 BUSINESS *Academic Disciplines* Entrepreneurship / Marketing / Social Media	Florida Teen Buys Houses	1: Starting Out Mobile (article) 2: Keeping Your Customers (article)	*Key Skill* Scanning to preview a text *Additional Skills* Using your knowledge Understanding key vocabulary Reading for main ideas Working out meaning Making inferences Synthesizing	Expressing contrast Business and marketing vocabulary	

CRITICAL THINKING	GRAMMAR FOR WRITING	WRITING	ON CAMPUS
Building support for an argument	Future real and unreal conditionals	*Academic Writing Skills* Paragraph structure and unity Impersonal statements *Rhetorical Mode* Argumentative *Writing Task* Make and support an argument for what to do with an aging but culturally or historically significant building. (essay)	*Study Skill* Staying organized with group projects
Determining and applying criteria	Nonidentifying relative clauses Appositives	*Academic Writing Skills* Structuring a summary-response essay Writing a conclusion *Rhetorical Mode* Summary-response *Writing Task* Summarize criteria and then analyze a logo in terms of that criteria. (essay)	*Life Skill* Building an academic resume
Determining the seriousness of a problem	Impersonal passive constructions Passive for continuity	*Academic Writing Skills* Writing about problems Writing about solutions *Rhetorical Mode* Problem-solution *Writing Task* Describe a problematic online behavior and explain what you think should be done to prevent or eliminate it. (essay)	*Research Skill* Identifying reliable online sources
Analyzing advantages and disadvantages	Reductions of subordinate clauses	*Academic Writing Skill* Writing about similarities and differences *Rhetorical Mode* Comparison and contrast *Writing Task* Compare and contrast (a) two products or services regarding their potential as a mobile business or (b) the appropriateness of loyalty programs and subscription services for a product or business. (report)	*Study Skill* Prioritizing your time

UNIT	WATCH AND LISTEN	READINGS	READING SKILLS	LANGUAGE DEVELOPMENT	
5 PSYCHOLOGY *Academic Disciplines* Experimental Science / History / Neuroscience	Interview with the Founders of IDEO	1: Mental Illness and Creative Genius: Is There a Connection? (article) 2: The Creative Mind (article)	*Key Skills* Using graphic organizers to take notes Interpreting quotes *Additional Skills* Understanding key vocabulary Previewing Reading for details Making inferences Predicting content using visuals Reading for main ideas Synthesizing	Experimental science terminology	
6 CAREERS *Academic Disciplines* Business / Education / Information Technology	Vocational Training	1: The Skills Gap (article) 2: What Is the Value of a College Education? (article)	*Key Skill* Interpreting graphical information *Additional Skills* Predicting content using visuals Understanding key vocabulary Reading for main ideas Reading for details Identifying purpose Making inferences Synthesizing	Complex noun phrases	
7 HEALTH SCIENCES *Academic Disciplines* Globalization / Medicine	Superbugs	1: Superbugs (article) 2: The Globalization of Infection (article)	*Key Skill* Recognizing discourse organization *Additional Skills* Using your knowledge Understanding key vocabulary Reading for main ideas Reading for details Working out meaning Making inferences Scanning to predict content Synthesizing	Verbs and verb phrases for causation Word families	
8 COLLABORATION *Academic Disciplines* Business / Human Resources / Sports Management	Office Space	1: The Value of Talent (article) 2: The Perfect Work Team (article)	*Key Skill* Using context clues to understand terminology and fixed expressions *Additional Skills* Previewing Understanding key vocabulary Reading for main ideas Summarizing Reading for details Using your knowledge Working out meaning	Language for hedging	

CRITICAL THINKING	GRAMMAR FOR WRITING	WRITING	ON CAMPUS
Annotation Finding points of synthesis across sources	Complex noun phrases with *what*	*Academic Writing Skills* Citing quoted material Writing an explanatory synthesis *Rhetorical Mode* Explanatory synthesis *Writing Task* What is creativity? Explain the current understanding of this concept, synthesizing information from different sources. (essay)	*Study Skill* Managing high volumes of reading
Analyzing information in graphs and other figures	Active vs. passive voice to discuss figures	*Academic Writing Skill* Making a claim *Rhetorical Mode* Argumentative *Writing Task* What is a good choice for a career path with a secure future? (essay with graphical support)	*Research Skill* Types of sources for research
Analyzing causes and effects	Cause and effect: logical connectors	*Academic Writing Skill* Writing about causes and effects *Rhetorical Mode* Cause and effect *Writing Task* Choose one infectious disease and discuss the factors that may have contributed to its development and spread or could do so in the future. (essay)	*Life Skill* Applying to a degree program
Understanding audience and purpose	Acknowledgment and concession	*Academic Writing Skill* Anticipating counterarguments *Rhetorical Mode* Argumentative *Writing Task* Present your recommendations for assembling and organizing an effective team for a particular business or collaborative group. (report)	*Communication Skill* The dynamics of group work

HOW *PRISM* WORKS

1 Video

Setting the context

Every unit begins with a video clip. The videos serve as a springboard for the unit and introduce the topic in an engaging way. The clips were carefully selected to pique students' interest and prepare them to explore the unit's topic in greater depth. As they work, students develop key skills in prediction, comprehension, and discussion.

WATCH AND LISTEN

ACTIVATING YOUR KNOWLEDGE

PREPARING TO WATCH

1 Take this survey about your online security habits. Check (✔) your answers. Discuss your answers with a partner.

How safe do you feel …	Very safe	Safe	Not safe
1 sharing your address with someone?			
2 shopping online?			
3 sending private information to someone's phone?			
4 storing private information on your cell phone?			
5 keeping passwords stored on your computer or phone?			

2 Discuss the questions with your partner.

1 Does everyone have a right to privacy? Why or why not?
2 Do you think celebrities and other public figures give up their right to privacy when they become famous? Why or why not?
3 What can people do to better protect their privacy?

GLOSSARY

hack (v) to use a computer to get into someone else's computer system or other electronic device illegally

scandal (n) activities that shock people because they think they are very bad

breach (n) an act of breaking a rule, law, custom, or practice

virtual fingerprint (n) unique characteristics of a computer, file, or set of data

liable (adj) having legal responsibility for something

64 UNIT 3

2 Reading

Receptive, language, and analytical skills

Students improve their reading abilities through a sequence of proven activities. They study key vocabulary to prepare them for each reading and to develop academic reading skills. A second reading leads into synthesis exercises which prepare students for college classrooms. Language Development sections teach vocabulary, collocations, and language structure.

READING

READING 1

PREPARING TO READ

USING YOUR KNOWLEDGE

1 You are going to read an article about mobile businesses. Read the statements. Do you think they are true or false? Write *T* (true) or *F* (false).

_____ 1 It's easy to turn a hobby into a business.
_____ 2 It is cheaper to start a food truck than a restaurant.
_____ 3 It usually only costs about $3,000 to start a mobile business.
_____ 4 New food truck owners usually make a profit more quickly than new restaurant owners.
_____ 5 The number of mobile businesses is increasing.
_____ 6 Food trucks are just a small fraction of the mobile retail market.

UNDERSTANDING KEY VOCABULARY

2 Read the definitions. Complete the sentences with the correct form of the words in bold.

aspiring (adj) wishing to become successful
break even (idm) to earn only enough to pay expenses
component (n) one of the parts of something
fluctuate (v) to change frequently from one level to another
outweigh (v) to be greater or more important than something else
proposition (n) a proposal or suggestion, especially in business
revenue (n) the money that a business receives regularly
transition (n) a change from one state or condition to another

1 The price of oil has _____ dramatically since 2000, going from $40 a barrel to almost $150 then down to $30!
2 My friend came to me with an interesting business _____, but I think it sounds a little too risky for me.
3 My daughter is a(n) _____ chef in New York. She hopes to get a job in a famous restaurant.
4 The benefits of this medication _____ its potential risks.
5 One _____ of the course focuses on reading comprehension and the other focuses on listening skills.
6 It can take teenagers a long time to make the _____ into adulthood.
7 The first year, our business lost money, the second year it _____, and this year we made a profit.
8 Amazon's _____ in 2015 was over $100 billion ($100,000,000,000).

90 UNIT 4

ACADEMIC WRITING SKILLS

SKILLS

Writing about causes and effects

Academic writing often includes explanations for why something happens or the consequences of events, behavior, or decisions. The first involves an analysis of causes, whereas the second requires an analysis of effects.
- A causal analysis addresses causal factors in a situation or decision.
- An effect analysis addresses the consequences of an event or situation. These analyses may be chains; in other words, one cause may lead to an effect that causes another effect. The distinction between causes and effects is not always clear cut, as the effect of one situation can become the cause of another, and so on.

More complex pieces of writing may include both types of analysis.

PRISM Digital Workbook

1 Review the articles in this unit. Do they involve primarily an analysis of causes or effects?

a Reading 1 _____   b Reading 2 _____

2 Work with a partner. Complete the tasks, first following the examples (items 1–3), then on your own (items 4–6).

1 Climate change is primarily the result of human activity. It is having a serious impact on the Arctic. Review this list of the effects of climate change.
- Glaciers are melting: getting weaker and smaller.
- There's an increase in shipping and other commercial activities.
- Floating ice, an important habitat for polar animals, is disappearing.
- Arctic areas are more accessible to humans.
- Sea ice is melting.
- Strong Arctic storms are more frequent.
- Arctic animals, such as polar bears, have become endangered.
- The ocean is getting warmer.
- Storms are breaking up weak areas of glaciers.

2 Study this chain based on the information in Task 1 above. Develop another cause or effect chain using at least three of the facts from Task 1.

| higher ocean temp | → | more freq storms | → | breakup glcrs |

| more shipping | ← | more access |

176 UNIT 7

3 Writing

Critical thinking and production

Multiple critical thinking activities begin this section, preparing students for exercises that focus on grammar for writing and writing skills. All of these lead up to a structured writing task, in which students apply the skills and language they have developed over the course of the entire unit.

ON CAMPUS

MANAGING HIGH VOLUMES OF READING

SKILLS

One of the biggest shocks for many new college students is the amount of reading they have to do. There are ways to manage the workload, but it takes practice.

PREPARING TO READ

1 Work with a partner. What strategies for managing reading volume do you predict will be presented? Come back to check your predictions after you read the text.

_____ _____ _____

WHILE READING

2 Read the comments on the next page from an Academic Support Center discussion board thread about how to deal with a high volume of reading. Write *T* (true) or *F* (false).

_____ 1 Students should read every word of an assigned text.
_____ 2 You read differently for a class discussion than for a test.
_____ 3 It is good to read before you go to sleep because you are relaxed.
_____ 4 It can take some time to become good at the suggested strategies.
_____ 5 You can usually understand the main idea of a chapter by previewing it.
_____ 6 It is helpful to read the study questions in a textbook before doing the reading.

PRACTICE

3 Work with a partner. Discuss the questions.

1 Which strategies from the discussion board would be easiest for you to implement?
2 Which strategies from the discussion board would be most difficult for you to implement?

132 UNIT 5

4 On Campus

Skills for college life

This unique section teaches students valuable skills beyond academic reading and writing. From asking questions in class to participating in a study group and from conducting research to finding help, students learn how to navigate university life. The section begins with a context-setting reading and moves directly into active practice of the skill.

WHAT MAKES *PRISM* SPECIAL: CRITICAL THINKING

Bloom's Taxonomy

In order to truly prepare for college coursework, students need to develop a full range of thinking skills. *Prism* teaches explicit critical thinking skills in every unit of every level. These skills adhere to the taxonomy developed by Benjamin Bloom. By working within the taxonomy, we are able to ensure that your students learn both lower-order and higher-order thinking skills.

Critical thinking exercises are accompanied by icons indicating where the activities fall in Bloom's Taxonomy.

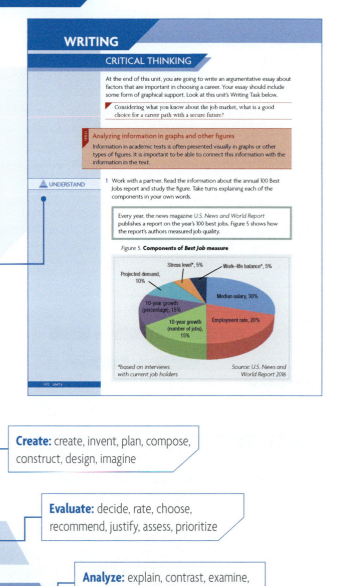

Create: create, invent, plan, compose, construct, design, imagine

Evaluate: decide, rate, choose, recommend, justify, assess, prioritize

Analyze: explain, contrast, examine, identify, investigate, categorize

Apply: show, complete, use, classify, illustrate, solve

Understand: compare, discuss, restate, predict, translate, outline

Remember: name, describe, relate, find, list, write, tell

WHAT MAKES *PRISM* SPECIAL: CRITICAL THINKING

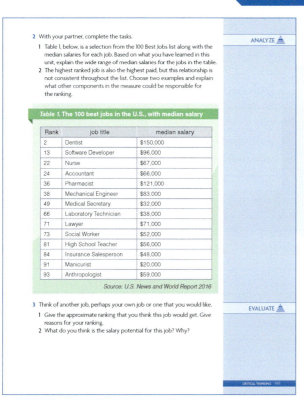

ANALYZE

2 With your partner, complete the tasks.

1 Table 1, below, is a selection from the 100 Best Jobs list along with the median salaries for each job. Based on what you have learned in this unit, explain the wide range of median salaries for the jobs in the table.

2 The highest ranked job is also the highest paid, but this relationship is not consistent throughout the list. Choose two examples and explain what other components in the measure could be responsible for the ranking.

Table 1. The 100 best jobs in the U.S., with median salary

Rank	job title	median salary
2	Dentist	$150,000
13	Software Developer	$96,000
22	Nurse	$67,000
24	Accountant	$66,000
36	Pharmacist	$121,000
38	Mechanical Engineer	$83,000
49	Medical Secretary	$32,000
66	Laboratory Technician	$38,000
71	Lawyer	$71,000
73	Social Worker	$52,000
81	High School Teacher	$56,000
84	Insurance Salesperson	$48,000
91	Manicurist	$20,000
93	Anthropologist	$59,000

Source: U.S. News and World Report 2016

3 Think of another job, perhaps your own job or one that you would like.

1 Give the approximate ranking that you think this job would get. Give reasons for your ranking.

2 What do you think is the salary potential for this job? Why?

EVALUATE

Higher-Order Thinking Skills

Create, **Evaluate**, and **Analyze** are critical skills for students in any college setting. Academic success depends on their abilities to derive knowledge from collected data, make educated judgments, and deliver insightful presentations. *Prism* helps students get there by creating activities such as categorizing information, comparing data, selecting the best solution to a problem, and developing arguments for a discussion or presentation.

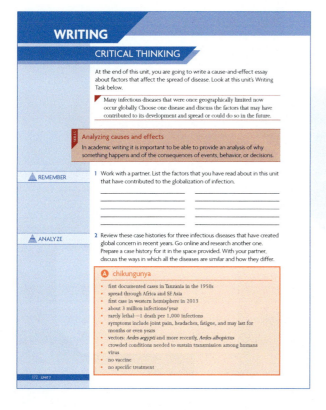

WRITING

CRITICAL THINKING

At the end of this unit, you are going to write a cause-and-effect essay about factors that affect the spread of disease. Look at this unit's Writing Task below.

Many infectious diseases that were once geographically limited now occur globally. Choose one disease and discuss the factors that may have contributed to its development and spread or could do so in the future.

Analyzing causes and effects

In academic writing it is important to be able to provide an analysis of why something happens and of the consequences of events, behavior, or decisions.

REMEMBER

1 Work with a partner. List the factors that you have read about in this unit that have contributed to the globalization of infection.

ANALYZE

2 Review these case histories for three infectious diseases that have created global concern in recent years. Go online and research another one. Prepare a case history for it in the space provided. With your partner, discuss the ways in which all the diseases are similar and how they differ.

A chikungunya

- first documented cases in Tanzania in the 1950s
- spread through Africa and SE Asia
- first case in western hemisphere in 2013
- about 3 million infections/year
- rarely lethal—1 death per 1,000 infections
- symptoms include joint pain, headaches, fatigue, and may last for months or even years
- vectors: *Aedes aegypti* and more recently, *Aedes albopictus*
- crowded conditions needed to sustain transmission among humans
- virus
- no vaccine
- no specific treatment

Lower-Order Thinking Skills

Apply, **Understand**, and **Remember** provide the foundation upon which all thinking occurs. Students need to be able to recall information, comprehend it, and see its use in new contexts. *Prism* develops these skills through exercises such as taking notes, mining notes for specific data, demonstrating comprehension, and distilling information from charts.

WHAT MAKES *PRISM* SPECIAL: ON CAMPUS

More college skills
Students need more than traditional academic skills. *Prism* teaches important skills for being engaged and successful all around campus, from emailing professors to navigating study groups.

Professors
Students learn how to take good lecture notes and how to communicate with professors and academic advisors.

Beyond the classroom
Skills include how to utilize campus resources, where to go for help, how to choose classes, and more.

Active learning
Students practice participating in class, in online discussion boards, and in study groups.

Texts
Learners become proficient at taking notes and annotating textbooks as well as conducting research online and in the library.

⊙ LANGUAGE DEVELOPMENT

EXPERIMENTAL SCIENCE TERMINOLOGY

Read the summary of a child development study. Write the words and phrases in bold next to their definitions below.

PRISM Digital Workbook

A study that began in 1986 **established a causal link** between the behavior of parents and the success of their children. The **research subjects** in this study were the families of 129 children living in poverty in Jamaica. There were two **experimental groups**, and each group received a different treatment. In one, the children received extra food and milk. In the other, the families received visits from an expert in early childhood development, who encouraged the parents to spend more time engaged with their children: reading books, singing songs, or simply playing. A third set of families, the **control group**, received no treatment. The experiment lasted for two years, but the researchers who **conducted the study** continued to follow the children.

The researchers found that the **intervention** that made the most difference in the children's lives was early parental interaction. As they were growing up, the children in this group exhibited more positive behavior and had higher IQ scores than the children in the other groups. As adults, they earn 25% more than the other participants in the study. The researchers **contend** that their results have clear **implications**. To ensure the future success of children living in poverty, educate parents about the importance of parent–child interaction.

1 _____ (v phr) to do academic research, such as an experiment
2 _____ (n) action taken to deal with a problem
3 _____ (n) conclusions suggested by the results of an academic study
4 _____ (n phr) participants in an experiment who do not receive experimental treatment
5 _____ (n phr) participants in an experiment who receive experimental treatment
6 _____ (n) all the participants in an experiment
7 _____ (v phr) to show a cause-and-effect connection
8 _____ (v) to claim

LANGUAGE DEVELOPMENT 123

Vocabulary Research

Learning the right words

Students need to learn a wide range of general and academic vocabulary in order to be successful in college. *Prism* carefully selects the vocabulary that students study based on the General Service List, the Academic Word List, and the Cambridge English Corpus.

GRAMMAR FOR WRITING

COMPLEX NOUN PHRASES WITH *WHAT*

A complex noun phrase with *what* can perform the same function as a noun + relative clause.

In a complex noun phrase beginning with *what*, the pronoun *what* replaces both the relative pronoun and the noun (phrase) it refers to. However, *what* can only be used to replace general terms like "the things/stuff/activities that ..."

These complex noun phrases can appear as subjects or objects. Notice that, although "the things/stuff/activities" are plural, *what* always takes a singular verb.

Subject: **What most people think of as creativity** generally involves divergent thinking.

Object: The quiet environment and free time gave him exactly **what he needed** in order to think creatively.

Complex noun phrases with *what* add variety to a writer's sentences. This structure is also an efficient and elegant way to draw attention to a point.

PRISM Digital Workbook

1 Rewrite the sentences so that they contain a complex noun phrase with *what*. Make sure to use the correct verb form after *what*.

1 The articles describe the activities that the research subjects in the study did in order to demonstrate their creativity.
_____

2 The things that have long been considered signs of mental illness may actually be part of the creative process.
_____

3 We still don't know for certain the things that lead to creativity.
_____

4 The researchers were looking for the things that single out the most creative people in the population.
_____

5 One of the goals of the study was to find out the activities that creative people are doing when they come up with their best ideas.
_____

126 UNIT 3

Grammar for Writing

Focused instruction

This unique feature teaches learners the exact grammar they will need for their writing task. With a focus on using grammar to accomplish rhetorical goals, these sections ensure that students learn the most useful grammar for their assignment.

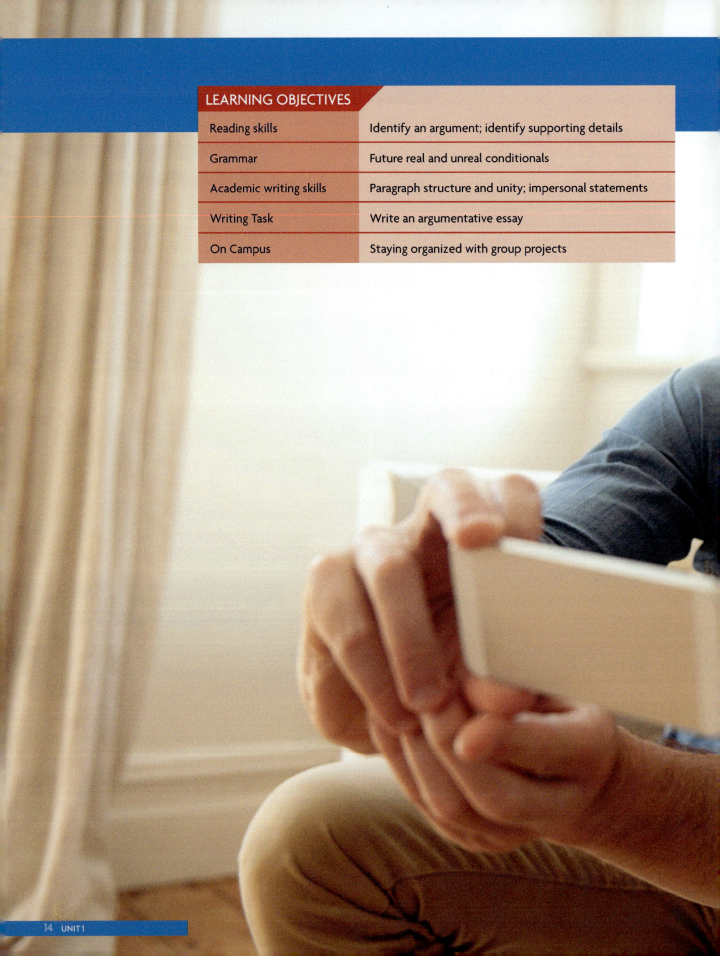

LEARNING OBJECTIVES

Reading skills	Identify an argument; identify supporting details
Grammar	Future real and unreal conditionals
Academic writing skills	Paragraph structure and unity; impersonal statements
Writing Task	Write an argumentative essay
On Campus	Staying organized with group projects

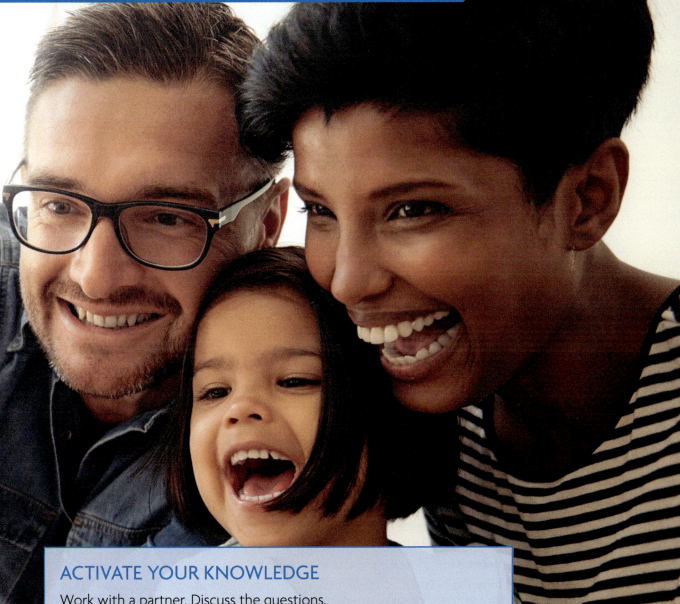

ACTIVATE YOUR KNOWLEDGE

Work with a partner. Discuss the questions.

1 Do you like looking at old family photos or old letters and postcards? Who keeps these things? How do they keep them (in photo albums, in a shoebox, in boxes in the attic)?

2 Do you like to visit old buildings or museums that show something about our past? Why or why not?

3 How important is it to preserve the past: buildings, records, art? Is preserving the past more important than creating new things?

PREPARING TO WATCH

1 Work with a partner. Discuss the questions.

1 Do you own a collection of music or movies? Is it stored on discs in your home or in a digital download folder on your computer?

2 Do you still have any CDs or DVDs? How long do you think they will last?

3 What could you do to preserve your CDs and DVDs? What other belongings do you have that might need to be preserved?

2 Look at the pictures from the video. Discuss the questions with your partner.

1 What problem do you think the woman is investigating?

2 Why do you think it is a problem?

3 What do you think will be learned by the research the woman is doing?

GLOSSARY

Library of Congress (n) the national library of the United States

posterity (n) the people who will exist in the future

parchment (n) the skin of animals that was used in the past to write on, or a paper made to look like this

degrade (v) to reduce the quality of something

longevity (n) how long a person or group of people lives, or how long a physical thing generally lasts; lifespan

Sharpie (n) a brand of permanent marker pen

WHILE WATCHING

3 ▶ Watch the video. Which sentence best expresses the main idea of the video?

1 ☐ The Library of Congress is testing the longevity of CDs every three to five years.

2 ☐ CDs are being aged to help learn which type of manufacturing is best for CD development.

3 ☐ How a CD is manufactured, how it has been handled, and how it has been stored all affect its longevity.

UNDERSTANDING MAIN IDEAS

4 ▶ Watch the video again. Write a detail for each main idea.

1 Fanella France and her colleagues are studying the preservation of CDs.

_____

2 To test CD durability, the Library of Congress is accelerating aging.

_____

3 There are several things people can do to preserve their CDs at home.

_____

UNDERSTANDING DETAILS

5 Work with a partner. Discuss the questions.

1 Why is it important for the Library of Congress to understand CD preservation?

2 What other items might the Preservation Research and Testing department of the Library of Congress be researching and testing?

3 What kinds of conditions might negatively affect old books, CDs, films, etc.? How might they go about testing these items under different conditions?

MAKING INFERENCES

DISCUSSION

6 Discuss the questions with your partner.

1 France offered suggestions on ways to preserve your CDs. Do you follow any of her suggestions? Will you pass the advice along to anyone else? If so, who?

2 What are some other items that are usually preserved in national libraries or museums?

3 Is there value in preserving items in their original format? Why not transfer the information to a new form of technology and discard the original thing?

4 Can we really learn from the past? Or do we learn just as much when we focus on the present and the future?

READING

READING 1

PREPARING TO READ

USING YOUR
KNOWLEDGE

1 You are going to read an article about storing records. Look at the list of information and records—in text, audio, and visual form—about your life. Add six more examples of your own. Then check where you store each type of thing. Compare your answers with a partner.

	in a box or drawer	on my phone/tablet	in the cloud	I throw them away.
old school records				
family photos				
bank statements				
selfies from vacation				
medical records				
receipts from major purchases				
music				

2 With your partner, discuss these questions.

1 Think about items in the chart in Exercise 1. How long do you think these records will last? Do you think your grandchildren will be able to access them? Your great-grandchildren? Why or why not?

2 Look at the title of the article on page 20. What does the word *digital* mean there? Give some examples of digital devices that you use. What are some digital devices that are no longer widely used—perhaps devices that your parents used?

3 The Dark Ages is the term used to refer to Europe from about the 5th to the 10th century. We have very few records from this time, so it is difficult to find out about how people lived then. How do you think *digital* could be related to *the Dark Ages*? What do you think the title means?

3 Read the sentences and write the words in bold next to the definitions.

1 The designers of the new phone have made a **deliberate** effort to make the device easy for anyone to use.

2 It is a common **practice** to name a baby after a parent or grandparent.

3 I am upset because my computer crashed, and I have not been able to **recover** the files on it.

4 We can't plan for everything, so we will have to handle problems as they **emerge**.

5 Your computer files are **vulnerable** if you don't protect them with a strong password.

6 All of the devices have the **capacity** to update information over Wi-Fi.

7 Problems with security **prompted** software designers to make major changes to the new version of the program.

8 The closet was filled with boxes of **memorabilia** from my childhood and my parents' early years of marriage.

a _____ (adj) not well protected; able to be harmed
b _____ (n) a regular or widespread habit or behavior
c _____ (v) to cause to do something
d _____ (v) to get something back
e _____ (n) ability
f _____ (adj) intentional
g _____ (n) a collection of items connected to a person or event
h _____ (v) to become known

Are We Living in the Digital Dark Ages?

1   Imagine these scenarios: (1) 2040: A box of **memorabilia**, including floppy discs and VHS tapes[1], is found in the attic of an old house with a label that says, "Records and early videos of Bill Gates (1975–1985)." (2) 2050: You find an envelope labeled "bank records" in your grandmother's desk. Inside the envelope, there is an old CD marked with the date 1998, your great-grandfather's name, and the words "all overseas bank accounts."

2   If these stories were really to happen, the people who found these items would be very excited—at least at first. Their excitement would be quickly followed by frustration because it would be very difficult for them to access the information on the discs and tapes. Even if the records were still in good condition, it would be very hard to find a device that could read them. Compare these discoveries to one that might have occurred around the turn of the twentieth century: a box of old letters and photographs on a high shelf at the back of a closet. The information these items contain would be immediately accessible because you would only need your eyes.

3   Computers and digital technology have vastly expanded our **capacity** to store all kinds of information, but how long will our access to this stored information last? In fact, the people who found the discs and tapes in our scenarios would be lucky because discs and tapes are physically real. Information on the Web is much more **vulnerable**; it is completely digital and can disappear in a flash. This is a problem that began to worry technology experts in the early 2000s. They became concerned

that, without better ways of preserving information, future generations might look back on our times as the "digital dark ages." If current **practices** continue, future generations may not have access to the digital record of our lives and our world.

4   Vint Cerf, a vice president at Google, argues that this could happen if we do not take steps quickly. He uses the term "bit rot" to describe how our digital records may slowly but surely become inaccessible. In our scenarios, for example, we may no longer have the devices, such as video and CD players, to access the records. Most software and apps that were used to create documents and websites ten or twenty years ago are already out of date, and in another sixty years they may not even be available. The problem is particularly challenging with interactive apps and websites. We can read letters from long ago, but will we be able to read a Twitter feed or access a Snapchat exchange a hundred years from now?

5   This problem has **prompted** technology experts like computer scientist Mahadev Satyanarayanan of Carnegie Mellon University to take action. He has found a way to store everything that is needed to interpret a record—the record itself as well as the original operating system and the application it used—all together in the cloud. Using this approach, he has been able to **recover** and preserve digital records that might otherwise have been lost forever.

6   Both Cerf and Satyanarayanan stress the importance of **deliberate** preservation. In the past, you could throw a bunch of photos into a box without having to decide what to save and what to throw away. With digital records, however, you need to make an active decision about what to keep. Satyanarayanan says it is likely that important records—government documents, big news stories, etc.—will be transferred to new forms of storage technology as they **emerge**. It is the records of everyday life, the ones we do not yet know we will value, that may disappear into the digital dark ages.

[1] **floppy discs and VHS tapes** (n) early forms of electronic media storage

WHILE READING

Identifying an argument

Most academic texts put forth an argument (or *claim*). It is important to be able to identify the central claim in a text and then to locate the evidence that the writer uses to support that argument.

4 Read the article. Then complete these tasks.

1 Which sentence best captures the writer's central claim?
   a Digital technology is not keeping up with the need to save records.
   b It would be easier to keep records if we made a physical copy of everything.
   c We are not preserving our digital records, so our history may be lost.
   d As our capacity to store records increases, we have to throw more things away.

2 Underline the sentence in the article that expresses this claim.

READING FOR MAIN IDEAS

PRISM Digital Workbook

5 Read the article again. Answer the questions with information from the article.

1 The writer begins with two examples to illustrate the central claim. What are they? Underline or highlight them in the article.

2 Reread Paragraph 4. What **two** problems with our current practices does Vint Cerf point out?
   a Physical records take up much more space than digital records. ☐
   b The devices necessary to read our records will not be available. ☐
   c Software used to create applications goes out of date quickly. ☐
   d We may not have access to the cloud in the future. ☐
   e It is not possible to preserve interactive applications such as Snapchat and Twitter. ☐

READING FOR DETAILS

6 Write *T* (true), *F* (false), or *DNS* (does not say) next to the statements.

_____ 1 Some early records of Bill Gates were recently found.

_____ 2 The capacity to store a lot of digital records does not guarantee future access to them.

_____ 3 Maintaining access to out-of-date interactive applications is particularly difficult.

_____ 4 Google is working on this problem and will reveal their solution soon.

_____ 5 Satyanarayanan has been working on this problem but has not been able to solve it.

_____ 6 All government records are currently stored in the cloud.

READING BETWEEN THE LINES

7 Work with a partner. Discuss the questions.

  1 In paragraph 1, the writer states, "the people who found these items would be very excited—at least at first." Why would they be excited?

  2 Why does the writer make a comparison to the Dark Ages?

  3 What do you think the term *bit rot* means? Think about the meaning of a *bit* in the digital world.

  4 Why is it more difficult to preserve a conversation thread on Twitter than a letter?

DISCUSSION

8 Work with a partner. Discuss the questions.

  1 Have you ever found a box of memorabilia? Describe what you found. How did you feel as you looked through it?

  2 The article talks about the need to make deliberate decisions about the kinds of records to save for future generations. What would you pick from your own life? From your family? From your community?

  3 Do you think it is important to save records of everyday life? Why or why not?

READING 2

PREPARING TO READ

1 Skim the reading texts on page 24 and answer the questions.

  1 What kind of texts are these?

  _____

  2 Who is the intended audience?

  _____

  3 Who wrote them?

  _____

  4 What do you think they will be about?

  _____

  _____

  _____

2 Read the sentences and choose the best definition for the words in bold.

1 The store that was once here closed five years ago, and the building
   has been **vacant** ever since.
   a busy
   b for sale
   c empty

2 We are looking for an **affordable** apartment, but everywhere we look
   the rents are too high.
   a not expensive
   b average
   c small but comfortable

3 **Developers** are going to build a shopping mall just outside of the city.
   a construction companies
   b companies that make a profit from buying and selling land
   c companies that buy land and build on it

4 The old building is falling apart, so the **renovation** is going to be very
   complex and expensive.
   a the replacement of an old building with a new one
   b the repair of a building to bring it into good condition
   c investment of money in an old building

5 The athletic **facility** at the university has a new ice-skating rink.
   a a building for a special purpose
   b a field
   c a place where people can meet

6 The government **maintains** that it has no money to pay for any new
   social programs.
   a continues to claim
   b finally understands
   c deeply regrets

7 The patient's condition has **deteriorated** rapidly. Doctors are doing
   their best to save her.
   a grown worse
   b stabilized
   c strengthened

8 After a period of adjustment, most immigrants find jobs and **prosper** in
   their new country.
   a stay
   b are successful
   c are optimistic

Dear members of the county board:

1   Cook County Hospital (CCH), which has been standing **vacant** for more than ten years, has become an eyesore[1] in our neighborhood. In spite of the fact that the government has spent millions of dollars studying the best use for the site, we are still waiting for action. Let's stop trying to figure out how to save this out-of-date pile of bricks. Our neighborhood is expanding and **prospering**, and it's about time for the board to show some leadership by adopting a proposal that embraces the future, not one that clings to the past.

[handwritten: refutation]

2   It has been argued that it would be cheaper to reuse the old building than to tear it down and build a new one. Almost ten years ago, experts estimated that saving the CCH building would cost more than 150 million dollars. This figure may have been true then, but over the last decade, the building has **deteriorated** considerably, which would no doubt add to the cost of any **renovation** carried out today. Our experts agree that updating this one hundred-year-old building to meet modern safety standards would actually be more expensive than starting from scratch[2]. *[handwritten: ① ②]*

3   What this neighborhood needs is an up-to-date, green structure that will provide much-needed housing and retail space. Our proposal will replace the decaying hospital building with a hotel, apartments (including 15% **affordable** housing), and space for stores, restaurants, and medical offices. Just as important, construction of these structures, and the businesses that will be located in them, will provide good jobs for people in the community. How much longer do we have to wait for our leaders to make the right decision for the future of our neighborhood? Tear down CCH!

Respectfully yours,
New Neighborhood Group

Dear Cook County Board:

1   Cook County Hospital, which welcomed patients and their families for almost a century, is a community landmark. The building is beautiful, but more beautiful than the structure itself is the statement it made to the city and the world. When it opened its doors in 1916, Cook County Hospital offered an attractive, modern **facility**, not just to the city's elite, but also to the poor. It sent the message that the poor are just as deserving of quality healthcare as the wealthy. People in the neighborhood called the hospital, *[handwritten: ①]* our *Statue of Liberty*. Let's make sure this site continues to serve all of our citizens by renovating it now. *[handwritten: appeal to emotion]*

2   Some opponents to our proposal have argued that renovation is too expensive, but a recent, similar project demonstrated that this may not be the case. In fact, renovating an existing structure can cost about $25 per square foot less than even the most basic new construction, while preserving the beauty of the original building. And, although it is often claimed that old buildings have a more significant environmental footprint[3] compared with new construction, architect and sustainability expert Carl Elefante **maintains** that the greenest building is the one that is already built. New construction almost always has a more serious environmental impact because it requires the use of all new materials.

3   Our group's proposal for renovation of the hospital site and building will allow it to continue to serve the community by providing affordable housing, medical clinics, a school, and a community center—resources that we badly need. If instead we allow **developers** to take over the project, the guiding principle will be profit, not neighborhood preservation. The people who will benefit most will be the investors in the project, not the people of our community. Save the Cook County Hospital building!

Respectfully,
Citizens Neighborhood Coalition

[1] **eyesore** (n) something ugly and unpleasant to look at
[2] **starting from scratch** (phr) starting over from the very beginning
[3] **environmental footprint** (n phr) the impact something/someone has on the environment

WHILE READING

3 Read the letters. Then complete these tasks.

READING FOR MAIN IDEAS

1 Which group makes the argument that the hospital should be <u>torn</u> down?
 ✓ **a** New Neighborhood Group
 b Citizens Neighborhood Coalition

2 Underline or highlight a sentence in the letter that expresses this argument.

3 Which group makes the argument that the hospital should be renovated?
 a New Neighborhood Group
 ✓**b** Citizens Neighborhood Coalition

4 Underline or highlight a sentence in the letter that expresses this argument.

Identifying supporting details

Writers support their arguments with details, such as reasons, explanations, or examples.

4 Read the letters again. Choose all the answers that are correct.

READING FOR DETAILS

1 What reasons does the New Neighborhood Group give to support its argument?
 Its proposal ...
 ✓**a** is cheaper.
 b has more community support.
 c can be completed more quickly.
 ✓**d** will provide jobs.
 e will last longer.

2 Underline or highlight these reasons in the letter.

3 What reasons does the Citizens Neighborhood Coalition give to support its argument?
 Its proposal ...
 ✓ **a** is cheaper.
 ✓**b** meets more of the community's needs.
 c is more popular with the community.
 ✓**d** is more practical.
 e is greener.

4 Underline or highlight these reasons in the letter.

READING BETWEEN THE LINES

5 Work with a partner. Discuss the questions.

1 Who do you think are the people behind the New Neighborhood Group? What are the group's goals generally?
2 Who do you think are the people behind the Citizens Neighborhood Coalition? What are this group's goals generally?
3 Why do you think Cook County Hospital was once compared to the Statue of Liberty?
4 What does the statement "the greenest building is the one that is already built" mean?

pytaj otic

DISCUSSION

6 Work with a partner. Use information from Reading 1 and Reading 2 to discuss the questions.

1 Do you think it is better to try to preserve old buildings or tear them down to make way for new ones? Would you give a different answer if the buildings were particularly beautiful or historically important?
2 Apart from the thing itself, what do you think is lost when something from the past disappears?
3 In the future, do you think we are more likely to lose physical or digital things?

⊙ LANGUAGE DEVELOPMENT

TIME EXPRESSIONS

There are many different phrases that can tell the reader when or how something happens. There are also phrases that describe things and events as they relate to a stated or implied timeframe.

when	how	in relation to a timeframe
at the turn of the century	slowly but surely	up to date
over the past / last + (week / month / year)	in a flash	out of date
at one time	in the blink of an eye	it's about time for
for the time being		

1 Complete the sentences with an appropriate expression. In some items, more than one answer is possible.

1 The clothes she wears are really _____ . People have not worn jackets like that since the 1980s.

2 _____ you to find a job. I am not going to support you any longer.

3 After a two-year downturn, _____ the economy is showing signs of recovery.

4 Twenty years ago, _____ , Twitter, Instagram, and Snapchat did not yet exist.

5 _____ this was the most popular restaurant in the city. Today, however, it's hardly ever full, even on Saturday nights.

6 I called the police and they got here _____ . I was surprised by how quickly they arrived.

7 If my company keeps doing well, we should be able to buy a house in the next couple of years, but _____ , we're renting an apartment.

8 _____ five years, the city has torn down more than ten historic buildings.

9 The owners have kept the building _____ with new lighting and an efficient heating system.

2 On your own or with a partner, complete the sentences with your own ideas using time expressions.

1 For the time being, I'm _____
_____

2 Slowly but surely, the world / country / city _____
_____

3 In order to stay up to date with technology, I _____
_____

4 In the blink of an eye, _____
_____

5 It's about time for me _____
_____

6 At one time, this _____
_____

COMPOUND ADJECTIVES

An adjective can be a single word or a phrase of two or more words acting as a single modifier. Depending on the type of phrase and its position in the sentence, the words may need to be hyphenated.

Before a noun, a compound adjective should be hyphenated.
We need more **up-to-date** reference materials.
My company just installed **state-of-the-art** graphics programs on all our computers.

When the same phrase appears in other contexts, no hyphenation is necessary.
I try to keep my software **up to date**.
This program was **state of the art** about ten years ago!

PRISM Digital Workbook

3 Circle the correct option to complete the sentences.

1 We need a more *long term / long-term* solution to this problem.
2 This city needs housing for *low income / low-income* families.
3 These homes were built at the *turn of the century / turn-of-the-century*, but they already need a lot of repair.
4 The neighborhood has implemented a system of *one way / one-way* streets to ease the increasing volume of traffic.
5 The artists in this area are quite *well known / well-known*.
6 Where there once were apartments, today most of the buildings are *single family / single-family* homes.
7 Appliances installed in newly constructed homes must meet strict government standards and also be *energy efficient / energy-efficient*.
8 As in any *fast growing / fast-growing* community, we face a number of challenges.

4 In your notebook, write five sentences using a compound adjective from the first column and an appropriate noun from the second column. Compare sentences with a partner. Did you choose the same word sets?

compound adjectives	nouns
low-income	homes / windows / light bulb
well-known	neighborhood / housing / apartments
long-term	author / song / story
energy-efficient	industry / city / business
fast-growing	goal / plan / care

WRITING

CRITICAL THINKING

At the end of this unit, you are going to write an argumentative essay in which you make and support an argument. Look at this unit's Writing Task below.

> Do some research to find an aging but culturally or historically important building in your city or country. What do you think should be done with it and why?

SKILLS

Building support for an argument

When you make an argument, you need to decide which facts are relevant and will support it.

1 Read these facts about preservation and new construction. Which support preservation (P) and which support new construction (NC)?

ANALYZE ▲

1 Renovation of old buildings in the state of Maryland kept 387,000 tons of building material out of landfills over a period of 12 years. That would fill a football field 60 feet high. _____

2 After a community is designated as a historic neighborhood, it is more difficult to make changes to buildings. As a result, the neighborhood becomes more stable, with fewer people moving out. _____

3 Some research studies estimate that a new, energy-efficient building can make up for the environmental impact of tearing down an old building in as little as ten years. _____

4 As buildings are renovated, higher-income people move in, demanding better schools and community services. _____

5 A recent study suggests that it takes 35–50 years for a new building to save the amount of energy that is used when an existing building is torn down and the new one is built. _____

6 A study in Delaware demonstrated that an average of 14.6 jobs were created per million dollars spent on renovation, compared with 11.2 jobs per million dollars spent on new construction. _____

7 When restoring old construction, there are often surprises that can cause a project to take twice as long as new construction projects, resulting in increased costs. _____

8 On a cost per square foot basis, renovation is usually slightly more expensive than new construction. _____

High Line Park, New York City

APPLY

2 Place the first five facts from Exercise 1 into the correct category. Then, based on what you learned in Reading 2, add one more category for the last three facts.

factor	fact
environmental impact	
community impact	
	6, 7, 8

EVALUATE

3 Work with a partner. Discuss which factors are most important to you when forming an opinion about a building's future and why. Brainstorm some ideas. Start with the list from Exercise 2.

1 Environmental impact: Will new construction save more energy than renovating the existing structure?
2 Community impact: How much would each option change the neighborhood?
3 _____

4 What other factors might be important (safety, tourism, duration, etc.)?

_____

GRAMMAR FOR WRITING

FUTURE CONDITIONALS

LANGUAGE

Both real and unreal conditionals can be used to make proposals about the future and to describe their consequences. The difference between them lies in how likely or certain it is that the event or action will take place.

Future real conditionals

Real conditionals imply a future event is possible or likely.
If we **tear down** the old city hall, we **will lose** our connection to the past.

Future unreal conditionals

Unreal conditionals imply a future event is unlikely, hypothetical, or impossible. This structure is often used to present alternative ideas or actions and their undesirable consequences.
If we **tore down** the old city hall, we **would regret** it.
If we **were to tear down** the old city hall, we **would regret** it.

1 Which statement describes an event that is more likely?

1 a If I spend much more time on my history project, I won't have time for my chemistry homework.

b If I were to start my history project all over again, I would choose a different topic.

2 a If I visited my parents this weekend, they would be really happy.

b If I visit my parents this weekend, I'll bring my laundry and do it there.

3 a If they hold the meeting in the community center, there won't be enough room for everyone to sit.

b If we were to hold the meeting today, not very many people would attend.

4 a If you left for the library, you might get there before it closes.

b If I leave for the library now, I might get there before it closes.

2 Write three sentences about the building you have chosen to discuss using the three forms of the future conditional in the explanation box.

1 (real conditional) _____

_____

2 (unreal conditional) _____

_____

3 (unreal conditional) _____

_____

ACADEMIC WRITING SKILLS

PARAGRAPH STRUCTURE AND UNITY

SKILLS

Academic essays are divided into unified paragraphs. Each paragraph should have a main idea. Paragraph *unity* means that the entire paragraph focuses on the main idea. The main idea is often, but not always, expressed by a *topic sentence*. All the other sentences in the paragraph provide background information or support for the main idea.

1 Read the sets of two sentences from a single paragraph. Decide which of the two would make a better topic sentence.   Irrelevant

1 ☐ a When a neighborhood becomes an officially recognized historic district, the people who own homes in this district benefit financially.

☐ b Homes in historic districts are worth approximately 25% more than similar homes in other areas.

2 ☐ a Fifty percent of visitors to Florida say they visited a historic site during their trip.

☐ b Historic sites increase tourism.

3 ☐ a Developers who renovate old buildings instead of tearing them down get a 50% reduction in their taxes.

☐ b Renovating an old building can be cheaper than building a new one.

4 ☐ a Prices usually rise when a neighborhood becomes a historic district.

☐ b Historic districts are usually not economically diverse because working class and even middle-class families cannot afford to live in them.

2 Decide whether each paragraph is unified. If the paragraph is not unified, cross out the information that does not belong.

1 unified ☐   not unified ☐

The creation of historic districts generally increases property values. Because their homes are protected, owners are willing to invest in them. Owners don't have to worry about future changes in the character and quality of their neighborhood. As a result, these districts tend to attract wealthier families who can afford to pay for the unique character that historic districts provide. However, higher property values make it difficult for families with less money to live in these areas.

2 unified ☐   not unified ☐

Many people believe that if they buy a home in a historic district, they will receive money from the government to make repairs. Unfortunately, this is not true, but they can get some assistance with their taxes. If they buy a home in a historic district and invest money to repair and preserve it, the local government will not increase the taxes on the home for eight years. They cannot make major changes that affect the appearance of their home without the approval of a committee that is in charge of the district. Owners can also apply for special federal funds to help keep their homes in their original condition.

3 unified ☐   not unified ☐

Farmers' markets are becoming increasingly popular in U.S. cities. In the past twenty years, their number has increased by about 125%. Farmers' markets are particularly popular in the Northeast, Midwest, and on the West Coast. Their popularity has been driven by the public's desire for locally grown food and also by an increasing awareness of the impact on the environment of food that comes from far away. Experts predict that the demand for locally grown food will continue to increase over the next ten years.

4 unified ☑   not unified ☐

The New York Historical Society, an organization dedicated to promoting research and public awareness of history and its influences on our lives today, was founded in 1804. It is the oldest museum in New York. Exhibits at the NYHS explore the rich cultural and social history of New York City, New York State, and the United States. It has a vast collection of items that <u>trace</u> the area's history to its very roots, including paintings of some of the country's most famous figures. It "It" overuse offers a $50,000 annual book prize for a work on U.S. history. Visitors to the NYHS will discover treasures including everything from famous works of art to the artifacts of everyday life in colonial times. ✓

IMPERSONAL STATEMENTS

When you state a position, there is no need to use phrases that mark it as your personal opinion such as *I think* or *we should*. The reader understands that you are making a case based on your view of the subject.

Instead of writing a personal statement:

In my opinion, The First National Bank should be torn down / restored.

Express the same idea with an impersonal statement:

The First National Bank has become an eyesore in our city, and the time has come to tear it down and replace it with a new building.

The First National Bank is of architectural and historical importance for our community and should be restored to its original beauty.

PRISM Digital Workbook

3 In your notebook, rewrite the sentences as impersonal statements. Compare sentences with a partner.

1 It is only my opinion, but I believe that city leaders did not act responsibly when they voted to allow construction on park land.

2 As far as I am concerned, it is always better to reuse and recycle the resources that we have instead of using up additional resources.

3 As I see it, a new convention center would be an incredible benefit for this city and its citizens, as it would provide both jobs and revenue. It would be foolish to pass up this opportunity.

4 It seems to me that by designating this neighborhood a historic area, we are telling all low-income homebuyers to stay away.

5 From my point of view, placing this building on the register of historic places is a step in the right direction because it has the potential to draw tourists who are interested in architectural and cultural history.

WRITING TASK

Do some research to find an aging but culturally or historically important building in your city or country. What do you think should be done with it and why?

PLAN

1 What building are you going to write about? Make note of its history, physical condition, and location. This information will be used in your introductory paragraph.

_____

_____

2 Do you think it should be renovated or torn down? Why? Write one or two sentences. This will be your thesis statement.

_____

_____

3 Look back at your notes from Exercise 3 in Critical Thinking. How do the different factors support your position? Write two or three ideas in a table like the one below. These will be the basis of your body paragraphs. Make notes that support your ideas.

	factor	notes
body paragraph 1		
body paragraph 2		
body paragraph 3		

4 What are some of the main alternative ideas? What would be the consequences of each? Use these points in your concluding paragraph.

_____

_____

5 Make notes on ways to restate your position to show that it is the best option. This is how you will end your essay.

_____

_____

6 Refer to the Task Checklist on page 35 as you prepare your essay.

WRITE A FIRST DRAFT

7 Use your essay plan to write the first draft of your essay in 500–600 words.

REVISE

8 Use the Task Checklist to review your essay for content and structure.

TASK CHECKLIST	✔
Does the introductory paragraph provide a good description of the building?	
Is your position definitely and clearly stated in your introduction?	
Do the body paragraphs offer support for your position from different angles (factors)?	
Do the body paragraphs state a proposal and its consequences?	
Does the concluding paragraph state the negative consequences of the alternative position?	
Is each paragraph unified?	
Does each paragraph include a topic sentence?	

9 Make any necessary changes to your essay.

EDIT

10 Use the Language Checklist to edit your essay for language errors.

LANGUAGE CHECKLIST	✔
Have you used time expressions correctly?	
Have you stated your proposal and its consequences with real conditional statements?	
Have you presented and dismissed alternative positions with unreal conditional statements?	
Have you expressed your opinions as impersonal statements, avoiding *I think, In my opinion,* etc.?	

11 Make any necessary changes to your essay.

ON CAMPUS

STAYING ORGANIZED WITH GROUP PROJECTS

 When students are working on a group project, keeping messages, files, and folders organized is important for every member of the group.

PREPARING TO READ

1 Work with a partner. Discuss the questions.

1 How organized are you?

very organized	both organized and messy	chaotic

mostly organized   mostly messy

2 Do you have a system for labeling your files or folders? What is it?

3 When you do a group project, how do you communicate with the others? How do you all edit the same document?

WHILE READING

2 Read a blog post from the team at the Writing Center about how groups can organize their work. Then complete the sentences below with information from the blog post.

1 The first thing that a group should do is decide on _____ _____ .

2 The group should choose a file-sharing system that everyone _____ .

3 Groups shouldn't use email for _____ .

4 A file name might include information such as _____ _____ .

5 When a file is revised, include something new at the end of the file name, such as _____ .

6 Instead of deleting old drafts, you should _____ _____ .

TEAMWORK: STAYING ORGANIZED AS A GROUP

by Chris Ryan

This week we want to talk about organizing your shared work when you're doing a group project.

First, choose a file-sharing system. There are a lot of choices: a learning management system (like Canvas), a social media site, an integrated platform (like Basecamp or Slack) where files, messages, and calendars are all in one place. Choose one that everyone has easy access to and is comfortable with.

For today's discussion, we'll look at communicating through email and a separate file sharing system.

EMAIL

- Use email for meeting times or task reminders, but not for sharing files.
- Be specific in the subject line. Instead of "Meeting" write "Meeting to review dataset 3."
- Make a special folder for the project. Keep all your emails about the project in that folder.

SHARED FILES & FOLDERS

- Choose a system for file sharing (like Dropbox or Google Drive).
- Decide on a system for naming files. When you revise, add a date, your initials, or numbers to the file name, for example:
  First draft by Nur Aydin:
    MOHAI_sample_NA.docx
  Revised by Manny Cruz:
    MOHAI_sample_NA_mc.docx
- Create folders for the different parts of the project (like Data, Photos, Interviews, Report).
- Create a folder called "Old Files" for first drafts and outdated material. This keeps the active folders clean and updated, and the old files handy for reference.

That's it! Come into the Writing Center if you need more help with organizing.

PRACTICE

3 In your groups, imagine you want to preserve a park in your city from development. You are doing research on the history of the area, interviewing residents, and taking photos. You will give a PowerPoint presentation and write a paper as a team.

1 How you will share files for this project?
2 What naming system for your files will you use? For revised files?

4 Now imagine you are the group leader. Write an email to the team to describe what you have all agreed on in Exercise 3. Share your emails within your group and offer each other feedback.

REAL-WORLD APPLICATION

5 Work with a small group. Research and compare three different file-sharing and collaboration platforms. Consider size of storage, how files are organized, if file sharing and communication are integrated, what kind of support there is, etc.

1 Choose the systems you want to compare. You can use the ones mentioned in the reading or your own favorite programs.
2 List of the main features of each one.
3 List two advantages and disadvantages for each one.
4 Share your work with another group and compare your results.

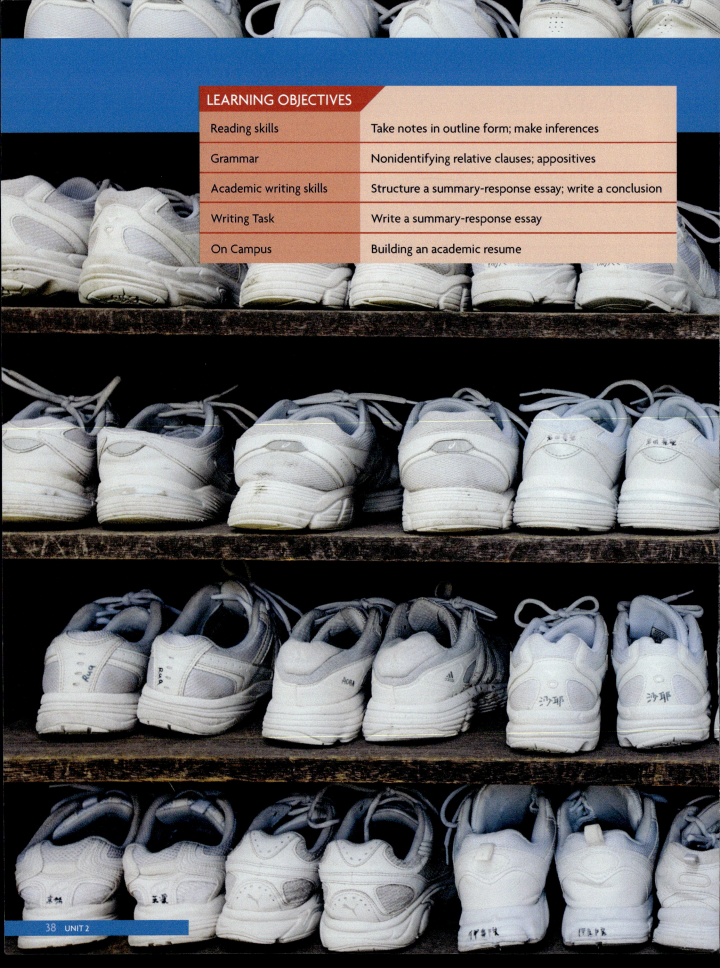

LEARNING OBJECTIVES

Reading skills	Take notes in outline form; make inferences
Grammar	Nonidentifying relative clauses; appositives
Academic writing skills	Structure a summary-response essay; write a conclusion
Writing Task	Write a summary-response essay
On Campus	Building an academic resume

ACTIVATE YOUR KNOWLEDGE

Work with a partner. Discuss the questions.

1 How many different brands of shoes are in this photo? Can you tell? Why or why not?

2 If you had to pick one pair of these shoes for yourself, which would you pick? Why would you pick that one over the others?

3 If the shoes all had a familiar logo, would it be easier to choose? What does a logo tell you about the product it is on?

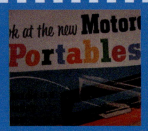   

PREPARING TO WATCH

1 Work with a partner. Discuss the questions.

1 What company logos are you familiar with? Describe the logos.
2 What makes these logos memorable?
3 Why do you think some logos are more memorable than others?

2 Look at the pictures from the video. Discuss the questions with your partner.

1 Which ads do you think are more effective? Why?
2 How does the look of the letters—the font—differ in each picture?
3 How do you think the font affects the look of a logo, ad, or sign?
4 Do you think the font affects the way people perceive the information? If so, how big a difference does it make?
5 What are the benefits of simple lettering?

GLOSSARY

endemic (adj) found particularly in a specific area or group

zany (adj) surprisingly different and a little strange, and therefore amusing and interesting

typography (n) the design of writing in a piece of printing or on a computer screen

Helvetica (n) a typeface or font that has clean, smooth lines

in full swing (idm) at the height of an activity

authoritarian (adj) demanding total obedience to

WHILE WATCHING

3 ▶ Watch the video. Which sentence best expresses the main idea of the video?

1 The ad for Coca-Cola is the most effective ad ever. ☐

2 Many corporations today use Helvetica because it communicates a clear message. ☐

3 Companies like to use Helvetica today so they appear strong and authoritarian. ☐

UNDERSTANDING MAIN IDEAS

4 ▶ Watch the video again. Write examples for each main idea.

1 In the 1950s, bad typography was prevalent.

_____

_____

2 Helvetica has several characteristics that make it successful.

_____

UNDERSTANDING DETAILS

5 Work with a partner. Discuss the questions.

1 Why do you think there was a wide variety of lettering designs in the 1950s?

2 How do you think the man feels about the use of exclamation points? How do you know?

3 Why do you think governments and corporations do not want to appear authoritarian?

4 Why do you think a corporation or government wants to appear accessible? How might that benefit consumers and citizens?

MAKING INFERENCES

DISCUSSION

6 Discuss the questions with your partner.

1 Which type of lettering do you prefer, the typography in the ads from the 1950s, or the ones of today? Why?

2 Do you think the lettering in an ad, logo, or sign is critical to the success of a business?

3 Is there an ad, logo, or sign that you find very attractive? Which one? Why do you think it appeals to you?

4 Is there an ad, logo, or sign that you find difficult to read or unpleasant to look at? Which one? What is the problem with it?

READING

READING 1

PREVIEWING

PRISM Digital Workbook

UNDERSTANDING KEY VOCABULARY

PREPARING TO READ

1 You are going to read a chapter from a marketing textbook about logos. Work with a partner. Preview the text and discuss these questions.

1 How would you answer the title question?
2 Would you say all of the logos in the text are successful? Why or why not?

2 Read the sentences and write the words in bold next to the definitions.

1 The judges used specific **criteria** to rate the performance of the athletes.
2 The initial report said that the business had made a 10% profit last year, but a **subsequent** report corrected the amount to 7%.
3 There are just a few news stories in the magazine; most of it is **devoted to** advertising.
4 My husband likes traditional art and furniture, but I prefer a more **contemporary** style.
5 The movie is quite violent, so it is not **appropriate** for young children.
6 Access to food and safe drinking water are both basic **human rights**.
7 The Red Cross is asking for **donations** of food and clothing to help victims of the earthquake.
8 The best way to **retain** good employees is to pay them a good salary.

a _____ (adj) existing or happening now
b _____ (n pl) fair and moral treatment that every person deserves
c _____ (adv) next; happening after something else
d _____ (n) money or goods given in order to help people
e _____ (n pl) standards used for judging something
f _____ (v) to keep; to continue having
g _____ (adj) correct or right for a particular situation
h _____ (adj) for one particular purpose

WHILE READING

READING FOR MAIN IDEAS

3 Read the textbook chapter. Then check (✔) the statement that gives the most complete and accurate description of a good logo.

a A good logo is easy for anybody to recognize and understand. ☐
b A good logo expresses a company's identity in a way that is easy to recognize. ☐
c A good logo will will last forever in the public's mind. ☐
d A good logo helps the company to make a profit. ☐

Chapter 5 — What Makes a Successful Logo?

1 In 2010, a group of world leaders got together to bring greater attention to **human rights**. They held a design competition for a logo that any organization **devoted to** human rights issues could use.

2 A logo is an efficient visual form that conveys an organization's message. Logos may seem rather simple. After all, they are often just a name or very basic image, but in fact, designing a good logo takes a lot of time and thought. So, what were the world leaders looking for? What are the **criteria** that define a good logo? If you ask ten different graphic designers, you may get ten different answers. However, there are some common themes.

3 A good logo is clear and simple. Simple logos are easy to remember. In studies where participants were shown hundreds of unfamiliar logos, the ones they remembered later all had simple designs. Some designers advise the use of no more than two colors.

4 A good logo must also be unique so it won't be confused with the logo from another organization. For example, the logo for IKEA is so familiar that any new

logo in those shades of blue and yellow would probably remind people of IKEA. A unique logo also arouses curiosity when people see it for the first time. They want to know more about it. When tennis star, Novak Djokovic began wearing shirts by the Japanese clothing manufacturer UNIQLO, people unfamiliar with the company became curious about the odd combination of letters that make up its logo.

5 Logos should be flexible enough to adapt across time and placement. We all remember Apple's rainbow-colored design, which worked in the 1970s, but today would look retro[1]. The **subsequent** gray and black Apple logo looks more **contemporary**, yet it **retains** the original design. Designers also need to consider where the logo will appear. Will it be on shopping bags? Coffee cups? Does it need to shrink down to a tiny icon on a digital device, like the Twitter bluebird or the Facebook **f**? Will people be able to recognize it from far away on the side of a truck?

6 More than anything else, a logo needs to tell a story—to convey the company's identity and evoke an emotional response in the people who see it. But to be successful, the message and the response must be **appropriate** for the organization that the logo represents. The Toys R Us logo, with its childish handwriting and backwards R, conveys a message of fun. It is childlike and playful. It works for a toy company, but it probably would not work for a bank or insurance company.

continue reading ▷

In contrast, the FedEx logo, with its block letters forming a forward-pointing arrow, looks like serious business. Its aim is to inspire confidence: We are a company you can trust your package to. An emotional response is particularly important for nonprofit[2] organizations. The World Wide Fund for Nature (WWF) hopes that its iconic black and white panda will resonate with the public and encourage people to make a **donation** to support its global environmental conservation work on saving the endangered species and their habitats as well as reducing people's footprint for a sustainable future.

7   Once a logo becomes widely recognized, businesses and organizations often rely more on the logo than their name. The public immediately recognizes the Nike swoosh, McDonald's golden arches, and Target's red and white circles because these logos have become so familiar.

8 So, what logo did world leaders hope would convey an immediately recognizable and unmistakable message of human rights? They chose Serbian designer, Predrag Stakić's logo, which combines the images of a bird and a human hand.

---

[1] **retro** (adj) having the appearance of something from the past
[2] **nonprofit** (adj) established for a reason other than making a profit, often for the arts, religious, or charitable purposes

Taking notes in outline form

Using an outline to take notes on a reading can help deepen your understanding of the reading and help you remember more of the details. Main ideas provide the basic organization for an outline, with supporting details listed underneath them.

4 Complete the outline with information from Reading 1. Fill in main ideas, details, and examples. Use examples from the text and add others that you are familiar with that also apply.

Criteria for a successful logo

I. Efficient form of visual communication
  A. simple and easy to remember
    1. Example: _____
    2. Example: _____
  B. _____ so it is unlikely to be confused with other logos.
    1. Example: _____
    2. _____
  C. arouse _____
    1. Example: _____
    2. Example: _____

II. _____ and adaptable
  A. across _____
    1. Example: _____
    2. Example: _____
  B. _____
    1. Can shrink
      Example: _____
    2. _____
      Example: _____

III. _____
  A. _____
    Example: _____
  B. _____
    Example: _____

READING BETWEEN THE LINES

Making inferences

Writers often suggest ideas but do not say them directly. In this case, readers need to *infer* what the writer means. Inferring meaning is an important reading skill. Readers combine what the writer says with logic and their own knowledge of the world to infer the complete meaning of the text.

PRISM **Digital** Workbook

5 Work with a partner. Go online and look at the UNIQLO logo. What about its design aroused so much curiosity, do you think? Write down some ideas.

_____

_____

IDENTIFYING PURPOSE

6 Think of three nonprofit organizations of different types and look up their logos. What kind of responses do you think they want to evoke with their logos? Are they successful?

nonprofit	response
1 _____	_____
2 _____	_____
3 _____	_____

7 Which of these logos would be most appropriate for a bank or insurance company? Why?

a **KeyBank** b c

DISCUSSION

8 Work in small groups. Discuss the questions.

1 Choose one of the logos discussed in Reading 1. What story do you think it is meant to tell?

2 Think of another logo. Choose one that you think is not as successful as those in Reading 1. Explain why you think so.

3 Do you think the human rights logo is successful? Look back at your outline for the criteria discussed in Reading 1. Give reasons for your answer.

READING 2

PREPARING TO READ

1 You are going to read another chapter in the textbook. Preview the reading on pages 48–49 and discuss the questions with a partner.

1 The chapter title uses the word *brand* to describe an action and adds the prefix *re-*. What do you think the process of *rebranding* involves?

2 Look at the images in this chapter. What role do you think logos might play in the rebranding process?

3 What are some of your favorite brands of casual clothing and shoes? How are the brands different from one another?

2 Read the sentences and choose the best definition for the words in bold.

1 There has been tremendous **opposition to** the new law requiring voters to show a photo identification card.
   a doubts about
   b disagreement with
   c misunderstandings about

2 The two sisters **resemble** each other so much that many people think they are twins.
   a look like
   b sound like
   c compete with

3 This clothing brand is designed to **appeal to** teenage women and girls.
   a send a message to
   b sell to
   c be interesting or attractive to

4 The community **resisted** the proposal to close our school for a long time, but we finally had to accept it.
   a tried to change
   b ignored
   c fought against

5 The government has **modified** its policy so that more people can apply for financial aid for college.
   a changed somewhat
   b renewed
   c started

6 Because I am trying to lose weight, I usually **opt for** water instead of soft drinks or juice.
   a refuse
   b choose
   c prefer

7 Many people **associate** specific foods with experiences in their childhood.
   a remember in a positive way
   b continue thinking about
   c make a connection in one's mind with

8 His role in the company has **evolved** over the past ten years. He began as a salesperson, but now he works with clients to build new products just for their needs.
   a become less useful
   b developed slowly
   c stayed the same

PREDICTING CONTENT
USING VISUALS

UNDERSTANDING
KEY VOCABULARY

PRISM Digital Workbook

Chapter 6   *Rebranding and Logos*

1   Businesses need to be able to change as markets change. To keep up with changes, they frequently update their brands and advertising in a process called *rebranding*. Rebranding often prompts these companies to redesign their logos at the same time. Take, for example, NBC (the National Broadcasting Company). This company started in the days of radio, thus the microphone in its original logo from 1944. As it moved into television and then color television, the company adopted its iconic peacock design in 1956. Since then, it has updated "the Bird" several times to reflect the tastes and styles of the times.

2   Rebranding and new logo designs may be needed because a company has changed its focus. For example, Xerox, a company whose primary product was once photocopiers, wanted to call attention to the fact that it handles a much wider range of document technology now. Some companies may want to change their image because there have been some negative associations with their old one. For example, the logo for oil company British Petroleum (BP) looked like any sign you might see at a gas station. Customers often **associate** gasoline with climate change and a negative impact on the

environment, so BP **opted for** a "greener" logo, one that **resembles** a sunflower. Kentucky Fried Chicken wanted to distance itself from unhealthy, fried foods. When it redesigned the product's logo, the word "fried" disappeared and only the initials KFC remained.

3   Some brands simply mature and need a new logo to show this. Many hi-tech companies, often founded by young entrepreneurs, begin with logos that reflect the age of their founders. If the companies are successful and begin to **appeal to** a wider audience, they may want to **modify** their logo. Both Spotify and Snapchat have gone through this process. Spotify's earlier, youthful logo has recently **evolved** into a simple graphic that evokes sound waves. Snapchat's cute ghost has lost its silly face, retaining only the figure's outline.

4   The public generally **resists** changes to familiar logos at first. However, **opposition to** the new design usually dies down after a while, especially if the new logo retains some familiar elements. For example, the new BP logo kept the color scheme of the old logo, and the new KFC logo retains the brand's familiar bearded face of its founder, Colonel Sanders. If there is too much change, however, customers may become confused or reject the change. Executives at PepsiCo found this out when they changed the logo for one of their brands: Tropicana orange juice. Customers were looking for the familiar orange with a straw; they did not recognize the product

with the new logo as Tropicana. Sales dropped dramatically, and Tropicana brought back the old logo.

5 A final reason for a new logo design comes from technology. New platforms[1] may necessitate modifications. As devices become smaller, logos need to be simpler and easier to recognize on a small scale. Companies like Airbnb and PayPal dropped their names and chose simpler graphics for their latest logos so that users can identify them more easily on their mobile devices.

6 Changes in technology can place limits on logo designs, but they can also offer new options. In particular, as more business and personal interactions take place in digital environments, more companies are creating logos that are animated and interactive. The foremost example of this is Google's new logo, which appeared in 2015. The new logo has the same four basic colors as the old logo, but it transforms into a number of different images, depending on the product. For example, at the start of a Google voice search, the logo transforms into four dots in the Google colors, then into four wiggling lines that look like sound waves.

7 New logos can be expensive. The sunflower logo cost BP close to $200 million, and Tropicana lost $33 million on its new logo. Yet, for most companies, the process can inject new energy into a brand, and is therefore considered worth the investment.

[1]**platform** (n) the type of system a computer or smartphone uses

WHILE READING

READING FOR MAIN IDEAS

3 Read the textbook chapter. Then check (✔) all the circumstances that might prompt a company to redesign its logo.

a The company wants to appeal to younger consumers. ☐
b Changes in technology require it. ☐
c The public does not like the old logo. ☐
d The company wants the public to forget about something negative. ☐

READING FOR DETAILS

4 Match the reasons for a logo redesign to the company.

1 need to fit logo on mobile devices
2 company and founders have matured
3 wider range of products
4 opportunities provided by new technology
5 negative associations
6 need to refresh look over time

a British Petroleum
b Google
c Snapchat
d Xerox
e NBC
f PayPal

Outlines do not always need to be formal, with numbers, letters, and single words. You can use a less formal organization to take more extensive, but less formal notes.

5 Read the textbook chapter again. Take notes using the informal structure below. Compare your notes with a partner.

I. Change in focus

_____

_____

_____

II. Brand has matured

_____

_____

_____

III. Problems with rebranding

_____

_____

_____

IV. Impact of changing technology

_____

_____

_____

READING BETWEEN THE LINES

6 Work with a partner. Choose the statement(s) that can you infer from Reading 2. Discuss your reasoning.

a A peacock is immediately associated with the idea of color.
b The founders of Spotify were young when they started the company.
c The new BP logo was a success.
d The face on KFC's logo is an important element of the brand.
e Other companies now have animated logos like Google's.

DISCUSSION

7 Work with a partner. Use ideas from Reading 1 and Reading 2 to discuss the questions.

1 How important do you think a logo is for a brand?
2 Give an example of your response to a specific logo. Do you think other people share your response?
3 Choose one of the pairs of logos discussed in Reading 2. Why do you think the company made the change?
4 Think of a famous logo, perhaps for a car, a clothing company, or a fast food restaurant. What changes would you suggest to improve the logo?

DESCRIBING EMOTIONAL RESPONSES

1 Study the table of common verb+noun collocations used to describe emotional responses. Do these expressions describe positive, negative, or mixed responses?

PRISM **Digital** Workbook

verbs	nouns	response
evoke	feeling(s), memories, emotions	a mixed
inspire	confidence, awe, fear	b
arouse	interest, curiosity, suspicion, anger	c
stir up	trouble, opposition, feelings, anger	d
generate	interest, excitement, enthusiasm	e
provoke	response, controversy, outrage, anger, anxiety	f

2 Complete the sentences with an appropriate collocation. In some items, more than one answer is possible.

1 The man wore a hat pulled down over his eyes and a large coat that seemed to be covering something. His appearance immediately _____ .

2 The new law that requires non-citizens to carry a special identity card at all times has _____ .

3 The new line of computer products and accessories has _____ a lot of _____ among tech-savvy buyers.

4 With his strong positions and years of experience, the presidential candidate _____ among voters.

5 The insults against the rap singer _____ an angry _____ from his many fans.

6 Songs from the past often _____ happy _____ .

3 Write three sentences of your own using some of the collocations in the table in Exercise 1 to describe emotional responses.

1 _____

_____

2 _____

_____

3 _____

_____

PARAPHRASING

Paraphrasing is an important and useful writing skill, especially when you write a summary. When you paraphrase, you put another person's ideas into your own words. To write a paraphrase, use synonyms and different grammatical structures to express the ideas in a new form without changing their meaning. You may also need to arrange the ideas in a different order.

Changes in technology can place limits on logo designs, but they can also offer new options.

At the same time that emerging technology restricts logo designs, it can also open up new possibilities.

If you use identifiable phrasing from the original text, you must use quotation marks.

PRISM Digital Workbook

4 Paraphrase the sentences.

1 Logos are symbols commonly used by companies and other organizations to promote their identity and to increase public recognition.

_____

_____

2 Many companies choose logos that reflect their names, origins, or products so that consumers can easily associate the logo with the company.

_____

_____

3 Color is a crucial element of any logo because colors help anchor the logo in consumers' memories, allowing them to distinguish the logo from other, similar logos.

_____

_____

4 Logos of sports teams, found on clothing, souvenirs, and other merchandising products, are a major source of revenue for teams.

_____

_____

5 Paraphrase three sentences from Reading 1 that describe the criteria for a successful logo.

1 _____

_____

2 _____

_____

3 _____

_____

WRITING

CRITICAL THINKING

At the end of this unit, you are going to write a summary-response essay. Look at this unit's Writing Task below.

> Summarize Reading 1, "What Makes a Successful Logo?" Then choose a logo that is not mentioned in either reading text and analyze it in terms of the criteria given in Reading 1.

SKILLS

Determining and applying criteria

Understanding criteria can help you organize an essay and ensure that you address the most relevant issues.

1 Review your outline of the criteria for a successful logo given in Reading 1 (pages 43–44). Write a list of the top criteria below.

1 _____
2 _____
3 _____
4 _____
5 _____

2 Work with a partner. Take notes as you go.

APPLY

1 Choose a logo for your analysis. _____
2 Apply the criteria from the list you made in Exercise 1.

_____
_____
_____
_____
_____
_____

3 Does your logo meet each of the criteria completely, partly, or not at all?

3 With your partner, answer the questions.

EVALUATE

1 How successful do you think your logo is? Explain your answer.

_____
_____

2 Is your judgment based on the criteria in the chapter or were other criteria important in your judgment? What were they?

_____
_____

NONIDENTIFYING RELATIVE CLAUSES

LANGUAGE

Writers use nonidentifying relative clauses to provide additional information about a noun clause. These details are not essential because the clause can be removed without affecting the sense of the sentence.

IKEA, **which is a multinational company,** has a logo that is recognized around the world.

PRISM Digital Workbook

1 Rewrite the sentences to include the additional information.

1 Apple's logo has been redesigned several times in the past forty years.
Additional information: The logo was once rainbow-colored.

_____

_____

_____

2 The letters in the logo for FedEx form an arrow moving forward.
Additional information: FedEx provides delivery services.

_____

_____

_____

3 A Serbian designer, Predrag Stakić, won the international competition.
Additional information: His design encapsulated the features of a dove and a hand.

_____

_____

_____

4 Rebranding is only one of many options available to the marketing department.
Additional information: Rebranding is a process that can revive interest in a company's products.

_____

_____

_____

5 High-tech companies have realized that they need to reconsider and revise their logos.
Additional information: High-tech companies often have very young founders.

_____

_____

_____

APPOSITIVES

LANGUAGE

An appositive is a noun phrase that renames or further identifies the noun that it follows. Like nonidentifying relative clauses, appositives provide additional information, but in appositives both the relative pronoun and the *be* verb are omitted. Commas set off the appositive phrase.

IKEA, a multinational company, has a logo recognized around the world.

Appositives are very common with proper nouns. They usually appear after the proper noun but can also appear before it. (Notice that when they appear before it, no commas are required, and the article is often omitted.)

Novak Djokovic, the tennis star, wears UNIQLO shirts.
Tennis star Novak Djokovic wears UNIQLO shirts.

PRISM **Digital** Workbook

2 Rewrite the sentences using the additional information as an appositive. Where possible, rewrite the sentences in two different ways. Then, write two sentences of your own with appositives, using the proper nouns given.

1 The golden arches have achieved international recognition as a symbol of fast food.
Additional information: The golden arches are McDonald's logo.

_____

2 The design of logos requires careful thought and preparation before they are released.
Additional information: Logos are a company's public face.

_____

3 Rupert Murdoch has announced he will turn over his media empire to his son next year.
Additional information: Rupert Murdoch is a media mogul.

_____

_____

4 Microsoft has lost some of its market share to Google in the past five years, and the trend continues with the latest software release.
Additional information: Microsoft is a software giant.

_____

_____

5 Kanye West

_____

_____

6 Amazon.com

_____

_____

SKILLS

Structuring a summary-response essay

There are two basic formats for a summary-response essay.

- Format 1: Summarize then respond. Summarize the entire source text first. Then respond with your own ideas or an application of the ideas from the source.
- Format 2: Integrate the summary and the response. Summarize the source text point by point, responding to each point with your own ideas or an application of the ideas from the source.

Remember that the *summary* should include only the most important points, not details. The *response* usually consists of impersonal statements of the writer's point of view, followed by support of that point of view.

PRISM **Digital Workbook**

1 Work with a partner to summarize the second paragraph of Reading 2. Then, on your own, write a response to that summary, in one or two sentences.

2 Work on your own. Summarize the fourth paragraph of Reading 2. Add a response, again in one or two sentences.

3 With your partner, compare your summaries and responses.

SKILLS

Writing a conclusion

The conclusion is your opportunity to make a final impression on your readers—to remind them of the point you are trying to make and to leave them with something to think about. As you write your conclusion, consider the question, "So what?"

Do ...

✔ refer to your main idea and emphasize its importance, without repeating your thesis statement.

✔ refer to something in your introduction; for example, if you began with a story, you could come back to it in your conclusion.

✔ give your readers something to think about:
  - point out wider implications of the ideas you have presented.
  - point out the personal relevance to your readers of the ideas you have presented.
  - refer to future possibilities.

Don't ...

✘ repeat your thesis or summarize your supporting points. In a very long essay, this might be appropriate, but it is not necessary in a short essay like the one you will write in this unit.

✘ undermine your argument with expressions such as "This is only one interpretation."

4 Work with a partner to complete the task.

1 Review the main idea activities after the two readings in this unit. Use them to help you write one sentence that expresses the main idea of each text.

"What Makes a Successful Logo?" (pages 43–44)

Main idea: _____

"Rebranding and Logos" (pages 48–49)

Main idea: _____

2 Read the last paragraph of Reading 1 again. Underline the phrase that refers to the main idea of the full text. Circle any parts of the paragraph that leave the reader with something new to think about.

3 Read the final paragraph of Reading 2 again. Underline the phrase that refers to the main idea of the full text. Circle any parts of the paragraph that leave the reader with something new to think about.

WRITING TASK

Summarize Reading 1, "What Makes a Successful Logo?" Then choose a logo that is not mentioned in either reading text and analyze it in terms of the criteria given in Reading 1.

PLAN

1 Which format will you use for your summary-response essay, format 1 or format 2 (see Academic Writing Skills, page 56)? _____

2 What logo will you discuss in your essay (see Critical Thinking, Exercise 2, page 53)? If possible, include a picture of it in your essay as a visual reference for your reader. _____

3 Review your list of criteria (see Critical Thinking, Exercise 1, page 53). Paraphrase each point here and use your paraphrases in your essay.

_____

_____

_____

_____

_____

4 Review the information that applies to the format you will follow.

FORMAT 1: SUMMARY AND THEN RESPONSE

Opening paragraph: Review the main idea that you wrote (Academic Writing Skills, Exercise 4) and use it as the basis of your one-paragraph summary of Reading 1. Make sure you have explained the criteria.

Body paragraphs: Write one or more paragraphs applying the criteria for a successful logo to your choice of product or service.

- Add details from Reading 2 if they are relevant to your essay.
- Review your notes on the application of the criteria to the logo you have chosen (see Critical Thinking, Exercises 2 and 3). You probably will **not** need a separate paragraph for each criterion.
- Refer to the criteria you wrote about in your introduction, but do not explain them again here.

Logo X is indeed simple but not unique, so it may easily be confused with other, more famous logos.

Conclusion: Make sure your conclusion answers this question: *After considering all of the criteria, do you believe the logo you selected is successful? Why or why not?*

FORMAT 2: INTEGRATED SUMMARY AND RESPONSE

Opening paragraph: Review the main idea that you wrote (Academic Writing Skills, Exercise 4) and use it as the basis of your opening paragraph.

Body paragraphs: Write one or more paragraphs explaining and applying each of the criteria for a successful logo to your choice of product or service. If there are any additional criteria that you think are important, discuss them as well.

Conclusion: Make sure your conclusion answers this question: *After considering all of the criteria, do you believe the logo you selected is successful? Why or why not?*

---

5 Refer to the Task Checklist on page 59 as you prepare your essay.

WRITE A FIRST DRAFT

6 Write your summary-response essay based on your essay plan. Write 500–600 words.

REVISE

7 Use the Task Checklist to review your essay for content and structure.

TASK CHECKLIST	✔
Does your essay contain a summary of the criteria—either in a separate paragraph (format 1) or point by point (format 2)?	
Does your summary include the most important information from the original textbook chapter?	
Did you use your own words to paraphrase the points in the original texts?	
Did you apply the criteria from Reading 1 to a new logo?	
Does your conclusion contain an evaluation of the logo's success?	
Have you left your reader with something to think about?	

8 Make any necessary changes to your essay.

EDIT

9 Now use the Language Checklist to edit your essay for language errors.

LANGUAGE CHECKLIST	✔
Have you used words and phrases for describing emotional responses correctly?	
Have you paraphrased any information pulled from Reading 1 and Reading 2?	
Have you used quotation marks and cited your source if you used the exact words from a source text?	
Did you set off the extra information in nonidentifying relative clauses with commas?	
Did you punctuate appositives correctly according to how each one is used?	

10 Make any necessary changes to your essay.

ON CAMPUS

BUILDING AN ACADEMIC RESUME

SKILLS

Many university applications require an academic resume, especially for graduate programs. This is an opportunity to show what your strengths are and how your experience has prepared you to achieve your goals.

PREPARING TO READ

1 Work with a partner. Discuss the questions.

   1 A resume is usually for the purpose of finding a job. Have you ever written a work resume? What information did you (or would you) include?
   2 What do you think admissions officers, rather than employers, would be interested in knowing about you?

WHILE READING

2 Read the handout on page 61 from an academic counselor about how to build an academic resume. Then categorize each piece of advice according to the reading. Make a chart like the one below in your notebook.

abbreviate	provide your email address
exaggerate	include unpaid work experience
be very detailed	provide your social security number
include small jobs	include activities that aren't at school
include your birthday	provide dates of everything
ask someone to read it	

Do ...	Don't ...

PRACTICE

3 Work with a partner to answer the questions so that they are true for you.

   1 What is your academic goal? Write one sentence to describe your goals.
   2 What work, including volunteer work or internships have you done? Write a brief description of your role and responsibilities.
   3 What extracurricular activities have you done? How did you participate?
   4 What honors or awards have you received?

ACADEMIC RESUMES

An academic resume is used for admission to universities and colleges as well as for scholarship applications. When creating your academic resume, keep these points in mind:

- Be honest. Don't lie or exaggerate[1].
- Be brief but clear. Try to limit it to one page.
- Don't use abbreviations the reader may not know. Write the words out.

- Include things that are impressive. Leave things out that aren't.
- Have someone read and proofread your resume.

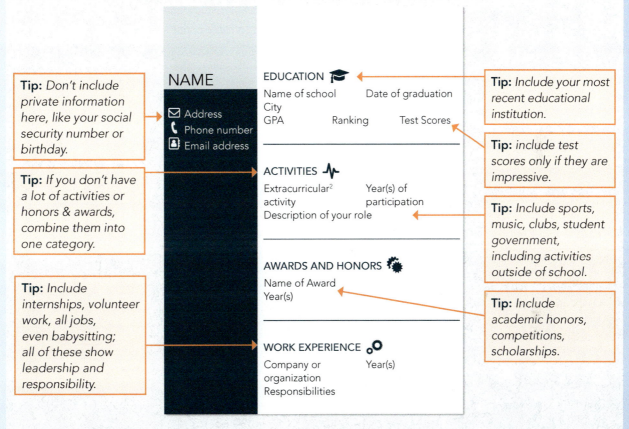

Tip: *Don't include private information here, like your social security number or birthday.*

Tip: *If you don't have a lot of activities or honors & awards, combine them into one category.*

Tip: *Include internships, volunteer work, all jobs, even babysitting; all of these show leadership and responsibility.*

NAME

☑ Address
☎ Phone number
📇 Email address

EDUCATION 🎓

Name of school
City
GPA   Ranking

Date of graduation

Test Scores

ACTIVITIES 〰

Extracurricular[2]   Year(s) of
activity   participation
Description of your role

AWARDS AND HONORS ✹

Name of Award
Year(s)

WORK EXPERIENCE ⚙

Company or   Year(s)
organization
Responsibilities

Tip: *Include your most recent educational institution.*

Tip: *include test scores only if they are impressive.*

Tip: *Include sports, music, clubs, student government, including activities outside of school.*

Tip: *Include academic honors, competitions, scholarships.*

[1]**exaggerate** (v) to make something seem more important than it is
[2]**extracurricular** (adj) for a school activity that is not part of academics

REAL-WORLD APPLICATION

4 Build your academic resume. Ask someone to read and proofread it for you. Make whatever changes are needed.

5 As a class, hold a resume fair to share your resumes. Incorporate the good ideas of others into your resume. Then write a final version.

Reading skill	Identify purpose and tone
Grammar	Impersonal passive constructions; passive for continuity
Academic writing skills	Write about problems; write about solutions
Writing Task	Write a problem-solution essay
On Campus	Identifying reliable online sources

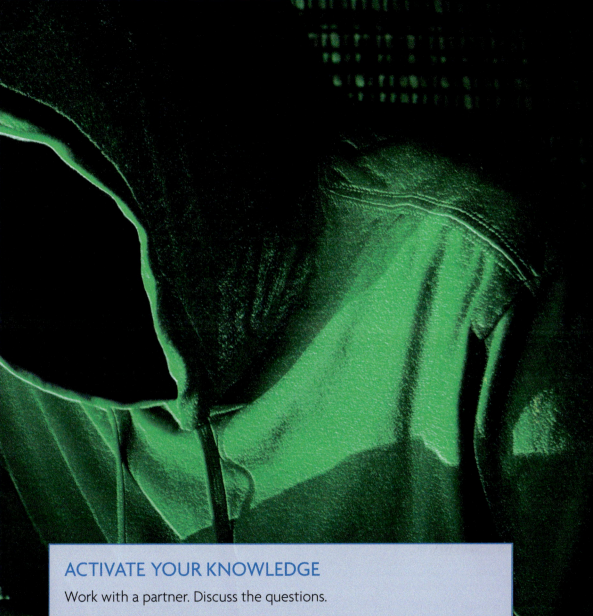

ACTIVATE YOUR KNOWLEDGE

Work with a partner. Discuss the questions.

1 How much time do you spend on the Internet every day? What sites do you spend the most time on?

2 In what ways do you interact publicly on the Internet other than social media? For example, do you post videos or comment on others' videos, comment on articles, review restaurants?

3 Do you know everyone you interact with online? How easy is it to communicate with total strangers?

   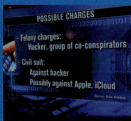

PREPARING TO WATCH

ACTIVATING YOUR KNOWLEDGE

1 Take this survey about your online security habits. Check (✔) your answers. Discuss your answers with a partner.

How safe do you feel ...	Very safe	Safe	Not safe
1 sharing your address with someone?	☐	☐	☐
2 shopping online?	☐	☐	☐
3 sending private information to someone's phone?	☐	☐	☐
4 storing private information on your cell phone?	☐	☐	☐
5 keeping passwords stored on your computer or phone?	☐	☐	☐

2 Discuss the questions with your partner.

1 Does everyone have a right to privacy? Why or why not?
2 Do you think celebrities and other public figures give up their right to privacy when they become famous? Why or why not?
3 What can people do to better protect their privacy?

GLOSSARY

hack (v) to use a computer to get into someone else's computer system or other electronic device illegally

scandal (n) activities that shock people because they think they are very bad

breach (n) an act of breaking a rule, law, custom, or practice

virtual fingerprint (n) unique characteristics of a computer, file, or set of data

liable (adj) having legal responsibility for something

Handwritten notes:
= beg.
plea.
bargain

ti
ligate litigate
sue
lawsuit

liable
: be charged with the
crime

prosecuted as the

WHILE WATCHING

3 ▶ Watch the video. Write *T* (true) or *F* (false) next to the statements below. Correct the false statements.

_____ 1 Apple has taken responsibility for the breach of security.

_____

_____ 2 The FBI is looking into the case to see if they can identify the hackers.

_____

_____ 3 The people who posted the photos are not liable and cannot be charged with breaking the law.

_____

_____ 4 Many people feel these are cases of a sex crime.

_____

_____ 5 People expect to have privacy in their own surroundings.

_____

4 ▶ Watch the video again. Write details for each main idea.

1 These types of attacks include hackers having personal information.

_____

_____

_____

2 Celebrities' devices will be looked at to trace the hackers.

_____

_____

_____

3 The law includes penalties for hackers and for those who share the information hacked via the Internet.

_____

5 Work with a partner. Discuss the questions.

1 Why do you think hackers target celebrities?

2 What do you think motivates a hacker to invade someone's privacy?

3 How might a hacker learn a celebrity's answers to security questions?

DISCUSSION

6 Work with a partner. Discuss the questions.

1 Who do you think is responsible in hacking cases? Why?

2 Do you think the punishment given to Christopher Chaney was fair? Why or why not?

3 What are some ways to make a password more secure?

READING

PREPARING TO READ

1 Read the sentences and write the words in bold next to the definitions.

1 We **guarantee** that you will not find a cheaper price for this computer anywhere.

2 She felt deep anger and **humiliation** when she learned that her private emails and photos had been published on the Internet.

3 The children had experienced years of **abusive** physical and emotional treatment.

4 Several athletes had to **withdraw** from the game because of injuries.

5 She was in the hospital, so no one could doubt the **validity** of her excuse for missing the deadline.

6 She is extremely upset at the moment because she has just heard some very **disturbing** news.

7 The journalist claims that he received the information from an **anonymous** source. The person would not give his or her name.

8 This action was not only unacceptable, it also **violated** his basic human rights.

a _abusive_ (adj) bad and cruel; causing another person mental or physical harm

b _disturbing_ (adj) upsetting; causing worry

c _guarantee_ (v) to promise absolutely or legally

d _validity_ (n) reasonableness or acceptability

e _anonymous_ (adj) unidentified or unidentifiable

f _violate_ (v) to break, such as a law or agreement

g _humiliation_ (n) shame and loss of self-respect

h _withdraw_ (v) to stop participating

2 You are going to read an article about cyber harassment. Work with a partner to complete the task.

1 Use a dictionary to find the meaning of each part of the term.
cyber: _____
harassment: _____

2 Now explain to your partner what you think *cyber harassment* means.

It is useful to know something about the topic before you begin reading. Quickly reading the first sentence of each paragraph can give you a good idea of what the article will be about.

3 Preview the article by reading the first sentence of each paragraph. Check (✔) the topics you think will be discussed in the article. Compare answers with a partner. After you finish reading, come back to check your predictions.

a a comparison between online and face-to-face harassment ☐
b reasons why cyber harassment continues to occur ☐
c a description of cyber harassment ☐
d how victims can fight against people who harass them ☐
e a description of people who engage in cyber harassment ☐
f an explanation of the legal issues in cyber harassment ☐

WHILE READING

4 Read the article on page 68. Then read these statements and write *MI* (main idea) or *SD* (supporting detail). Which paragraph does each one apply to?

PRISM Digital Workbook

condese
condescending
misogynistic
所文.

intered. main idea

Statements	MI or SD	Paragraph
1 Complaints about cyber harassment by victims are sometimes considered too dramatic.	SD	5
2 Trolls engage in disruptive behavior for a variety of reasons.	MI	3
3 Forty percent of Internet users have experienced some form of cyber harassment.	SD	2
4 It is difficult to stop cyber harassment.	MI	~~5~~ 4
5 Victims of cyber harassment often do not get a lot of support.	MI	4
6 Cyber harassment takes many forms.	MI	2
7 Limiting offensive speech may be considered a violation of the right to free speech.	SD	4
8 Many Internet users experience cyber harassment.	SD	
9 Cyber harassment includes physical threats.	SD	2.
10 Trolls harass other Internet users because they enjoy causing pain.	SD	~~5~~ 3

5 In your notebook, use your work in Exercise 4 to create an outline of the article. Look back at page 45 for help.

CYBER HARASSMENT

1   Bloggers like Amanda Hess know about it. Journalist Caroline Criado-Perez is also familiar with it. Online gamer Jenny Haniver knows it all too well. They all know about cyber harassment because they have all been victims. Cyber harassment ranges from behavior such as name calling online to more **disturbing** behavior, including threats of violence, posting embarrassing photos, and spreading personal or false information online. In the most serious cases, as in those of Hess, Criado-Perez, and Haniver, the harassment continues over a long period of time, with numerous offensive and threatening posts every day.

Journalist Caroline Criado-Perez

2   A 2014 survey revealed that this kind of harassment is quite common. Almost three-quarters of all Internet users have seen it happen, and 40% have experienced it personally. It has been suggested that even these figures may not reflect the full extent of the problem. Cyber harassment is particularly common among younger Internet users, and women are more likely to experience its more serious forms. Criado-Perez made the suggestion online that the Bank of England should put more women on their banknotes. For this idea, she received hundreds of hostile comments against her personally and against women more generally. Haniver was the victim of ongoing **abusive** comments and threats for apparently no other reason than she was an assertive female gamer. Blogger Hess received similar treatment. You can easily find examples of cyber harassment on social media, in the comments section of many blogs and websites, and especially, in the online gaming world.

3   Who is saying and doing all of these nasty things and why? The worst behavior is believed to come from so-called *trolls*, Internet users who disrupt Internet communication with negative and offensive actions and comments. These individuals take pleasure in insulting other users, causing them **humiliation** and pain. Studies suggest that some of these people have mental or emotional problems; however, experts believe that many people who engage in online abuse are otherwise unremarkable people. Harassing others simply brings them the attention and excitement that their lives in the offline world may lack. The cover of the Internet allows them, and perhaps even encourages them, to behave in ways that they never would in face-to-face situations.

4   Victims of this kind of harassment often ask why trolls are allowed to remain **anonymous**. Shouldn't people who are abusing the system be made to answer for their conduct? Victims also wonder why someone—the government, Internet service providers, or the social networking sites themselves (e.g., Facebook, Twitter, etc.)—does not do more to stop such attacks. Although these points have **validity**, eliminating anonymity and limiting what people can say on the Internet present problems of their own. Many people prefer not to reveal their identity online, not because they are trolls, but because they want to protect their own privacy. For example, you may want to ask questions in a chat room about a health problem that you do not want others to know about. Furthermore, limiting what people can say online or anywhere else could set a dangerous precedent. It could be seen as **violating** the constitutional right to free speech which **guarantees** all people the right to say what they want, even if it is unpopular or offensive.

5   Because the harassment takes place online, it is not always taken seriously. A threat online may not seem as real as a threat that occurs face to face. Victims are often told not to be "drama queens." Yet, the impact of this harassment on its victims is very real and very damaging. They often suffer serious psychological shock and pain. They may lose their confidence and **withdraw** from all interaction on the Internet because they fear that they or their families will suffer abusive treatment in return. Recovery can be difficult, and for some, it never comes. For others, the experience prompts them to speak out. Jenny Haniver blogs, tweets, and speaks about her experiences of harassment in the world of gaming in hopes of bringing more public attention to this issue.

READING BETWEEN THE LINES

Identifying purpose and tone

Understanding the writer's purpose and his or her perspective on the topic can deepen your understanding of the material. Negative and positive words can help you determine if the writer is offering praise or criticism.

6 Work with a partner to complete the tasks.

1 Choose the idea that best describes the writer's main purpose in writing this article.

   a to stop cyber harassment

   b to change the laws that govern cyber harassment and behavior on the Internet

   c to inform readers about the problem of cyber harassment

   d to convince the government to punish people who engage in cyber harassment

   e to help the victims of cyber harassment

2 Choose the phrase that best describes the writer's tone regarding cyber harassment.

   a neutral and informative   *neutral*

   b positive, offering praise

   c negative, offering criticism

3 Skim the article. Find words and phrases that support your ideas about the writer's tone and highlight or circle them. Explain your choices to another pair of students.

belligerent.
=angry / upset
detached

tone.

troll 鄉蟲俠

DISCUSSION

7 Work in small groups. Discuss the questions.

1 Have you ever had an experience with cyber harassment, either directed against you or someone you know? What happened?

2 Do you think people should be allowed to post comments on the Internet anonymously? Why or why not?

3 Why do you think women are more likely to experience the most serious forms of cyber harassment?

4 What do you think you would do if someone started harassing you online?

PREPARING TO READ

1 You are going to read an essay about possible solutions to cyber harassment. Work with a partner. Discuss these questions.

1 The title of the essay is "Combatting Cyber Harassment." What kind of solutions to cyber harassment do you think it will offer?

2 What kind of advice do you think the essay will give to victims of cyber harassment?

3 Who do you think is responsible for stopping offensive behavior on the Internet?

2 Read the sentences and choose the best definition for the words in bold.

1 One of the players on the team was **suspended** for three games for hitting another player.
a required to pay money as a result of doing something wrong
b fired from one's job
c not allowed to participate in an activity for a period of time

In the game
on the team

punitive
|
punishment

2 The city announced it would **prosecute** anyone who disturbed the peace during the election. *prosecution*
a search for in order to arrest
b take to court to determine the guilt of
c commit a crime against

3 For weeks, he has been receiving **malicious** letters and phone calls, filled with lies that could destroy his career.
a legal but inappropriate
b untruthful *make up*
c intentionally hurtful

4 We will probably never be able to **eliminate** crime, but we can take steps to reduce it.
a remove; get rid of completely
b find an appropriate punishment for
c weaken significantly

mitigate

assemble

5 The research institute has **assembled** a team of top scientists in an effort to find the cause of the disease.

   (a) gathered   **b** attracted   **c** interviewed

6 The government imposes a **penalty** on people who do not pay their taxes on time.

   a law   (b) punishment   **c** permission

7 The government has just passed a set of laws to help **regulate** the growing online retail market.

   (a) control   **b** encourage   **c** tax

8 The inability to write well can be a **barrier** to professional success.

   a the answer   **b** the last step   (c) something that blocks access

   obstacle

   obstacle

WHILE READING

3 Read the essay on page 72. Match each main idea to the correct paragraph.

   a The online gaming community is taking steps to reduce abuse. _____
   b Legal measures have not been very effective. _____
   c We need to do more to fight abusive online behavior. _____
   d People are starting to take cyber harassment more seriously. _____
   e Online communities are beginning to make rules against cyber harassment. _____

READING FOR MAIN IDEAS

4 Read the essay again. Complete the table with the actions that each group is taking to combat cyber harassment.

READING FOR DETAILS

group	actions
online gaming communities	
Twitter	
Google	
federal and state governments	

Combatting Cyber Harassment

1   Cyber harassment can have a serious and destructive impact on its victims and their families. Yet, until recently, it was not taken seriously. Instead, it was widely believed that this behavior was similar to childish fights, but this attitude is changing. Media attention on several recent cyber harassment cases has prompted the public to demand that trolls be held accountable for their behavior. Additionally, as offensive and often **malicious** behavior has become more prevalent, and the threats by Internet trolls have become more frightening, social media apps and sites, as well as online gaming communities, are taking notice. They worry that their users will begin to abandon their sites if trolls are allowed to operate freely. In short, taking responsibility for cyber harassment has also become an economic issue.

2   The effort to combat cyber harassment requires a two-pronged approach: prevention and **penalties**; however, to date, most of the focus has been on the first. Prevention can be controversial. The anonymity of the Internet makes harassment easy, yet placing any limits on online interaction could threaten the benefits of both the anonymity and free speech that we value. Online gaming communities want to provide maximum freedom to their participants, but these are the places where a great deal of harassment occurs, especially of female players. To try to address this problem, one hugely popular gaming site, *League of Legends*, **assembled** a team of behavior experts to study its 67 million monthly users. What they discovered surprised them. They expected to find a small group of badly behaved players—users who were responsible for most of the abuse and hostile behavior. Their plan was to **suspend** these players in hopes of **eliminating**, or at least reducing online harassment. They did find a few "bad apples," but they discovered that most of the offensive behavior came from players who were usually good Internet citizens. They only acted badly occasionally. The research team had greater success when the chat function on the game was removed. This resulted in abusive comments dropping by 30%. This study suggests that creating even a small **barrier** to bad behavior can often stop abuse before it starts.

3   Other online communities and sites have already taken steps in this direction. Twitter has had a "report abuse" button since 2013. Some gaming sites have systems that allow players to establish their reputations in the same way that sellers on online market sites, such as eBay, must do. They rate one another as "good player" or "avoid me." In other words, the communities are beginning to **regulate** themselves. They are also using the latest technology to identify the worst offenders. Google has sponsored a research study to find an algorithm[1] for identifying them. Their posts are more frequent and generally contain negative words, poor grammar, and misspelled words, allowing researchers to identify and ban users who exhibit troll behavior.

4   Over the past few years, the federal government and about half the states in the U.S. have updated their laws to cover threats and stalking[2] over the Internet. Nevertheless, our laws still lag disturbingly behind emerging technology. What is more, so far, very few people have been **prosecuted** under the laws that do exist. Experts offer advice that is familiar to anyone who has been the victim of bullying: ignore it. Do not respond to the

harassment. By responding to it, you give the trolls what they want—attention. Although this is generally considered to be good advice, unfortunately it often does not stop ongoing abuse.

5   As we spend more and more time on the Internet, addressing offensive and threatening behavior online is becoming increasingly important. As Laura Hudson wrote in *Wired Magazine* in 2014, "… the Internet is now where we socialize, where we work. It's where we meet our spouses, where we build our reputations. Online harassment isn't just inconvenient, nor is it something we can walk away from with ease. It's abhorrent[3] behavior that has real social, professional, and economic costs."

[1]**algorithm** (n) a set of instructions to a computer
[2]**stalking** (n) illegally following someone over a period of time
[3]**abhorrent** (adj) morally wrong; evil

READING BETWEEN THE LINES

IDENTIFYING PURPOSE AND TONE

5 Work with a partner to complete the tasks.

1 What is the writer's purpose? Check all that apply.
   a to eliminate cyber harassment ☐
   b to inform readers about current steps to stop cyber harassment ☐
   c to tell readers about specific cases of cyber harassment ☐
   d to help victims fight against and recover from cyber harassment ☐
   e to convince readers that more must be done to stop cyber harassment ☐

2 Which phrase best describes the writer's tone regarding cyber harassment?
   a neutral and objective ☐
   b informative and argumentative ☐
   c negative and emotional ☐

3 Skim the article. Find words and phrases that support your ideas about the writer's tone and highlight or circle them. Explain your choices to another pair of students.

DISCUSSION

SYNTHESIZING

6 In small groups, use ideas from Reading 1 and Reading 2 to discuss the questions.

1 What advice would you give to a victim of cyber harassment?
2 Do you think technology will find the solution to the problem? How?
3 What kind of penalty do you think that people who in engage in cyber harassment should face?
4 Do your suggestions protect the benefits of anonymity described in Reading 1?
5 What do you think are the consequences of cyber harassment beyond its effect on victims?

COLLOCATIONS FOR BEHAVIOR

PRISM Digital Workbook

1 Complete each sentence with one verb (in the correct form) and one noun to describe behavior or responses to behavior.

verbs
build   exhibit   experience
lose   suffer   take

nouns
abuse   behavior   confidence   pain
a reputation   responsibility

1 When you have done something wrong, it is important to ___take___ ___responsibility___ for your actions.

2 My online service provider has ___built___ ___a repu___ for protecting its users from abusive behavior.

3 People who have ___ex___ ___ab___ online often decide to withdraw from any interaction at all on the Internet.

4 It is not only trolls who ___exhibit___ hostile and offensive online ___behavior abuse___. Some ordinary users have also been known to act badly.

5 The stress of online abuse can cause people to ___suffer___ ___abuse pain___ that is both physical and psychological.

6 Even a single hostile or abusive online post can cause a user to ___lose___ ___conf___ and feel bad about himself.

2 Choose three of the negative adjectives from the box and write sentences to describe online activity, behavior, comments, or posts.

abhorrent   disturbing   insulting   negative   threatening
abusive   hostile   malicious   offensive

1 _____

_____

_____

2 _____

_____

_____

3 _____

_____

_____

PROBLEM-SOLUTION COLLOCATIONS

There are many nouns and verbs that describe problems and solutions. Some form typical or frequent collocations.

	verbs	nouns
stating the existence of a problem	*become, face*	*an issue*
	face, pose, present, represent	*a challenge, a danger, a problem, a risk, a threat*
	cause, run into	*trouble, problems*
describing solutions	*address, confront, eliminate, face, respond to* **mitigate**	*a challenge, a danger, an issue, a problem, a risk, a threat*
	fix, resolve, solve	*a problem*
	resolve	*an issue*

3 Work with a partner. Read the scenarios. Retell each one to your partner, using the language in the chart to describe the problems and solutions.

PRISM Digital Workbook

> 1 Two neighbors both wanted to park their cars in a space next to their apartment building. They argued about it constantly. Neighbor A had a violent temper and frightened Neighbor B, who complained to the owner of the building. The owner decided to park his own car in the space so neither neighbor could use it.

> 2 In the past, passengers arriving at the Houston Airport complained constantly about the length of time they had to wait for their baggage. Airport officials tried several approaches to solve the problem, including hiring extra staff. With these adjustments, the wait time was reduced to about the average at most airports, but passengers still complained. Eventually, the officials decided on a more extreme solution. They moved the baggage claim area farther away, so passengers had to walk farther to reach it.

> 3 A city neighborhood was having a problem with rats. The rats lived on the garbage people had thrown out. The neighbors considered using poison, but they worried about pets or even children coming into contact with it. They tried traps, but the rats were too smart. One neighbor had read about an organization that brings feral cats (wild cats that live on the streets) into neighborhoods with rat problems. The neighbors contacted the organization which delivered five feral cats. A week later, the rats were gone. The neighbors don't think the cats killed all the rats, but those they did not kill were certainly scared away.

CRITICAL THINKING

At the end of this unit, you are going to write a problem-solution essay. Look at this unit's Writing Task below.

> Describe an online behavior that you think is a problem and explain what you think should be done to prevent or eliminate it.

EVALUATE

1 Work in small groups. Read the descriptions of negative or abusive online behavior. Look up any words you do not know. Rank each behavior as extremely serious (1), very serious (2), or somewhat serious (3).

_____ **cyberstalking**: the use of the Internet to engage in ongoing harassment, which may include threats, false accusations, gathering and posting personal information and images

_____ **identity theft**: using personal information found online to take another person's identity and use it for one's own benefit

_____ **abusive reviews**: excessively negative reviews written about a business with the goal of maliciously causing damage to it

_____ **cyberbullying**: humiliating individuals online and encouraging others to join in similar behavior

_____ **grooming**: establishing an emotional connection with a young person online in order to take advantage of him or her

_____ **cyber scamming**: the use of the Internet to engage in fraud

ANALYZE

2 In your group, discuss the questions and make note of good ideas that arise.

1 Which types of Internet behavior do you think will be easier to stop—more serious abuse or less serious abuse?

2 Choose two or three of the behaviors listed in Exercise 1. Who (which people or organizations) do you think should be responsible for preventing or responding to this behavior? What steps should they take to prevent or eliminate the behavior?

3 What could individual Internet users do to help in this effort?

4 What are some consequences for victims of allowing this behavior to continue? For Internet users generally?

GRAMMAR FOR WRITING

IMPERSONAL PASSIVE CONSTRUCTIONS

Writers often choose the passive voice when the agent—the one performing the action—is "people." As a subject, "people" may be too general or repetitive.

People say that cyber harassment is most common in the male-dominated online gaming world.

Good writers can solve this problem in two different ways:

- create a passive that has no apparent agent
  *Cyber harassment **is said to be** most common in the male-dominated online gaming world.*

- move the real subject into the next clause by using the passive with *it*
  ***It** is said that cyber harassment is most common in the male-dominated online gaming world.*

These passive constructions often appear with the verbs *agree, argue, believe, claim, consider, decide, expect, say, think,* and *understand.* Note, however, that not all of these verbs allow both constructions.

1 In your notebook, rewrite these sentences in the impersonal passive in two ways. For the last two items, only one of the constructions is possible.

PRISM Digital Workbook

1 People believe that these figures underestimate the size of the problem.
2 People claim that the trolls are responsible for the most abusive forms of cyber harassment.
3 People expect that victims of online harassment will speak out against their abusers.
4 People understand that self-regulation is the best way to control bad behavior.
5 People consider "Just ignore it" to be sensible advice to victims of online harassment.
6 People have argued that these problems will require a legal solution.

2 Now write three sentences of your own using an impersonal passive construction with *say, believe,* or *think.*

1 _____
_____
2 _____
_____
3 _____
_____

PASSIVE FOR CONTINUITY

One reason a writer might choose to use the passive is to maintain continuity of subject within and across sentences. In other words, the passive allows writers to continue using the same noun phrase as the subject in some form.

Because the **harassment** takes place online, people do not always take **it** seriously.

      subject of the clause   subject of   object of

                               the sentence   the sentence

Because the **harassment** takes place online, **it** is not always taken seriously.

      subject of the clause   subject of the sentence

In the second sentence, *harassment* is the subject of the dependent and main clauses, providing greater continuity. Notice that the *by* phrase is omitted.

PRISM Digital Workbook

3 Read the sentences. Rewrite the second clause or sentence using the passive. Omit the *by* phrase if it is not necessary.

1 Although the stalker had been harassing students for weeks, the police did not catch him until yesterday.

2 A full year after the plane disappeared over the Indian Ocean, the crew of a fishing boat saw pieces of the plane floating 25 miles from shore.

3 Coffee is one of Brazil's most important crops. Farmers grow most of it in the area along the Atlantic coast.

4 One week after Congress passed a bill to make cyber harassment illegal, the president signed it into law.

5 Polar bears and some other Arctic animals are in danger of extinction. Climate change has drastically reduced their habitat.

4 Read the paragraph. Underline all the instances in which the subject of one sentence appears in another role in subsequent sentences. Then rewrite the paragraph in your notebook using the passive where appropriate. Omit the *by* phrase if it is not necessary.

> Identity theft is a growing problem. It occurs when someone uses your personal information to open bank accounts, borrow money, or make purchases. Almost 17 million people reported identity theft last year. The elderly are especially likely to become victims. Criminals targeted over 2.6 million older people in 2014. Stolen credit cards were the most common source of identity theft. Unfortunately, police usually do not recover the stolen cards.

ACADEMIC WRITING SKILLS

Writing about problems

When presenting problems, writers use a range of strategies to demonstrate to their readers that these problems are important. Facts, statistics, and examples (especially ones that will resonate with readers) can highlight the seriousness of the problem. Writers may also offer an opinion, either overtly or implicitly.

Here are some examples of these strategies from the texts in this unit.

Facts (F):   Many states do not have laws against cyber harassment.

Statistics (S):   Almost two-thirds of all Internet users have encountered cyber harassment.

Examples (E):   Jenny Haniver was subjected to months of violent threats.

Opinions (O):   As we spend more and more time on the Internet, addressing offensive and threatening online behavior is becoming increasingly important.

                  Nevertheless, our laws still lag disturbingly behind emerging technology.

1 Read the statements and label the strategy the writer uses: *F, S, E,* or *O*.

PRISM Digital Workbook

1 Three-quarters of all cyberstalking victims are female. _____
2 After several abusive reviews, business at the hair salon decreased dramatically. _____
3 It is imperative that the police find and prosecute the people behind these online scams. _____
4 Most teens and children do not tell their parents when they experience cyberbullying. _____
5 Laura Hosmer lost her entire life savings when someone found her social security number and other personal information online. _____
6 Zoe quit school after months of cyberbullying by other students. _____
7 Because it involves children, grooming is one of the most abhorrent online behaviors. _____
8 In the past year, almost 16 million Americans were victims of identity theft. _____

2 Work in small groups. In your notebook, write four sentences with at least one fact, one statistic, one example, and one opinion about online behavior. Share your sentences with the class.

Writing about solutions

When a writer offers recommendations or solutions, they may do it in several ways:

- cite experts or research (R)
- cite generally held views (G)
- make direct suggestions of their own (S)

PRISM Digital Workbook

3 Read the statements and label the strategy the writer uses: *R*, *G*, or *S*.

1 A recent study suggests that that a minor change in a game's design can significantly reduce abusive behavior. _____
2 One solution is to require social media sites to do a better job of regulating their members' behavior. _____
3 These new, stricter laws are considered effective tools for combatting cyber scams. _____
4 Most Internet users prefer self-regulation to government intervention. _____
5 Technology presented the problem, so technology should also provide a solution. _____
6 Media professionals believe we need to provide more public support for victims and more penalties for trolls. _____

4 Work in small groups. Write two examples of each of these strategies. Share your sentences with the class.

R a _____

   _____

   _____

   b _____

   _____

   _____

G a _____

   _____

   _____

   b _____

   _____

   _____

S a _____

   _____

   _____

   b _____

   _____

   _____

WRITING TASK

Describe an online behavior that you think is a problem and explain what you think should be done to prevent or eliminate it.

PLAN

1 Use this chart to organize your ideas. First, write a statement of the problem you want to write about (negative online behavior) and its consequences. Then, brainstorm possible solutions. (Review your ideas in Critical Thinking, Exercise 2.)

problem	consequences

possible solutions	
1	6
2	7
3	8
4	9
5	10

2 Use your notes in the chart to write your introductory paragraph.

- Describe the problem.
- Explain its consequences.
- End with a thesis statement that suggests there are possible solutions, but do not list what those solutions are. You will present those in the body of your essay.

3 Think about your body paragraphs. Which two or three of the solutions in your chart do you think are most likely to be successful? Present one possible solution per paragraph.

- State a possible solution and explain how it works.
- Explain what steps need to be taken to carry out this solution.

Solution 1: _____

_____

_____

_____

Solution 2: _____

_____

_____

_____

Solution 3: _____

_____

_____

_____

4 Think about your concluding paragraph. Be sure to do the following:

- Refer back to your main idea.
- Emphasize the importance of acting against this behavior.
- Leave your readers with something to think about.

5 Refer to the Task Checklist on page 83 as you prepare your essay.

WRITE A FIRST DRAFT

6 Write your problem-solution essay based on your essay plan. Write 500–600 words.

REVISE

7 Use the Task Checklist to review your essay for content and structure.

TASK CHECKLIST	✔
Have you explained the negative online behavior and its consequences in your introductory paragraph?	
Does your thesis statement suggest that solutions are possible but not list them?	
Have you provided at least two possible solutions in separate body paragraphs?	
Do you refer to research or generally held views?	
Does each paragraph have a topic sentence, and are all points in the paragraph related to that topic?	
Does your conclusion refer back to the main idea of your essay?	

8 Make any necessary changes to your essay.

EDIT

9 Use the Language Checklist to edit your essay for language errors.

LANGUAGE CHECKLIST	✔
Have you used appropriate vocabulary to describe behavior and responses to behavior?	
Have you used problem-solution collocations?	
Have you used impersonal passive statements in your essay?	
Is there continuity of subject in your passive sentences?	
Have you used a mix of facts, statistics, examples, and opinions?	

10 Make any necessary changes to your essay.

When doing research online, it is vital that the sources you use are reliable and academically accepted. Knowing what to look for takes practice, but there are some clues to help you determine whether a site can be trusted.

PREPARING TO READ

1 Work with a partner. Preview the reading by looking at the headings. Answer the questions.

1 What types of sites are considered "unreliable sources"? What do they all have in common?
2 What types of sites are "reliable sources"? What do they have in common?
3 Why might a nonprofit site need investigation before deciding whether it is reliable?

WHILE READING

2 Read the poster on the next page about evaluating websites for reliability. Then match each website below with the description of it as a source.

1 blog   a may be interested in selling something
2 professional journals   b often provides opinion instead of facts
3 website ending in .gov   c authors often affiliated with universities
4 website ending in .com   d reliable source, but may not include author
5 website ending in .org   e requires more research on the group
6 website ending in .edu   f by professionals for others in same field

PRACTICE

3 Work with a partner. Which of these would be good sources for a paper on attitudes of young people about online privacy?

1 "Current trends in identity theft," from a website selling identity theft protection systems. ☐
2 A 2016 government report based on a survey about teenagers' awareness of privacy issues. ☐
3 A blog from a parent about protecting children online. ☐
4 "Millennials and privacy," from a nonprofit research group. ☐
5 "Youth privacy in a social world," from a journal for sociologists. ☐
6 An article on the reasons students overshare online, written by a professor from your college. ☐

FINDING RELIABLE SOURCES

Students need good sources for their research papers, but they often don't know how to find a reliable source.

UNRELIABLE SOURCES

Blogs: Anyone can write a blog. The writer may not be an expert or even have any real knowledge of the subject. Blogs often include biased information and personal opinions, not factual data or research.

Company websites: Sites that end in ".com" are commercial sites. These sites may provide information for customers, but they are often designed to sell products or services. These sites may present a biased point of view.

Wikipedia: Many different people contribute to the pages of Wikipedia. The writers are not necessarily experts in the field. Students should never use Wikipedia as a source, but there are a few ways that Wikipedia may be useful in your research: you can get general background information on your topic, find key words to do other searches, and find reliable sources in their list of resources.

RELIABLE SOURCES

Educational sites: Sites that end in ".edu" are typically reliable sources. People that contribute to these sites are often professors or researchers. Articles on these sites are based on studies and research.

Government sites: Websites that end in ".gov" can be trusted. They often present data or statistics from government agencies. Often, there is no author for these sources, but they are written by experts.

Online professional journals: These sources are based on research and present balanced information. The articles are written by professionals for other people in their field.

Newspapers: Newspapers respected for their accuracy and balanced reporting are good sources.

SITES THAT NEED MORE RESEARCH

Nonprofit sites: A website that ends in ".org" is nonprofit. Nonprofit organizations include groups like the Red Cross, an international relief organization. However, they can also include groups who have a religious or political bias. Always do your own research to learn more.

OTHER SOURCES

Article and research databases: The college subscribes to over 200 databases of research, data, and scholarly articles. With your student ID, you can use these databases and find good, reliable sources. A reference librarian can show you how to find the right database.

REMEMBER THAT THE LIBRARIANS ARE ALWAYS HERE TO HELP YOU.

REAL-WORLD APPLICATION

4 With your partner, imagine you are writing a paper on the attitudes of young people about online privacy. Find some reliable sources.

a one government source: _____

b one educational source: _____

c one news source: _____

LEARNING OBJECTIVES

Reading skill	Scan to preview a text
Grammar	Reductions of subordinate clauses
Academic writing skill	Write about similarities and differences
Writing Task	Write a comparison and contrast report
On Campus	Prioritizing your time

ACTIVATE YOUR KNOWLEDGE

Work with a partner. Discuss the questions.

1 Are there a lot of food trucks and other mobile businesses where you live? Do you ever buy from these businesses?

2 What makes you choose to shop at one business instead of another?

3 If you were going to start your own small business, what would it be? Give reasons for your answer.

PREPARING TO WATCH

ACTIVATING YOUR
KNOWLEDGE

1 Work with a partner. Discuss the questions.

1 What are typical things that teenagers like to do?
2 What are some of the ways that teenagers can earn money where you live?
3 Do you know a teenager who owns a business? What kind of business?

PREDICTING CONTENT
USING VISUALS

2 Look at the pictures from the video. Discuss the questions with your partner.

1 What activities do you think the teenage girl likes?
2 What kind of business do you think she has?
3 How much money do you think she earns?

GLOSSARY

foreclosure (n) the act of taking back property that was bought with borrowed money because the money was not paid as agreed

garage sale (n) an occasion when people sell things they no longer want but feel someone else might want; often done in a garage

attention deficit hyperactivity disorder (ADHD) (n) a condition in which someone, especially a child, is often in a state of activity or excitement and unable to direct their attention toward what they are doing

deed (n) a legal document that is an official record and proof of ownership of property

take stock (idm) to examine a situation carefully

WHILE WATCHING

UNDERSTANDING MAIN IDEAS

3 ▶ Watch the video. Check (✔) the ideas you hear.

1 Willow is a landlord. ☐
2 Willow has sold furniture and other items to earn money to buy houses. ☐
3 Once Willow is a legal adult, all the properties will belong to her. ☐
4 Willow has a goal of owning 10 houses by the time she is 18. ☐
5 Willow plans to become a realtor. ☐

UNDERSTANDING DETAILS

4 ▶ Watch the video again. Write a detail for each main idea.

1 Willow made a good deal of money selling furniture, allowing her to buy her first home.

_____

2 Her goal is to buy two houses a year.

_____

3 Willow's mother is helping her.

_____

4 Willow participates in many tasks as a landlord and business owner.

_____

MAKING INFERENCES

5 Work with a partner. Discuss the questions.

1 What do you think Willow is learning as a landlord and business owner?
2 Why do you think Willow wanted to start a business?
3 Why do you think her mother is so proud of her?

DISCUSSION

6 Discuss the questions with your partner.

1 How would you describe Willow? Why?
2 What could other teenagers learn from Willow?
3 If you started a business as a teenager, what kind of business would it be?
4 What are some advantages and disadvantages of entering into business so young?

READING

READING 1

PREPARING TO READ

USING YOUR KNOWLEDGE

1 You are going to read an article about mobile businesses. Read the statements. Do you think they are true or false? Write *T* (true) or *F* (false).

_____ **1** It's easy to turn a hobby into a business.

_____ **2** It is cheaper to start a food truck than a restaurant.

_____ **3** It usually only costs about $3,000 to start a mobile business.

_____ **4** New food truck owners usually make a profit more quickly than new restaurant owners.

_____ **5** The number of mobile businesses is increasing.

_____ **6** Food trucks are just a small fraction of the mobile retail market.

UNDERSTANDING KEY VOCABULARY

2 Read the definitions. Complete the sentences with the correct form of the words in bold.

> **aspiring** (adj) wishing to become successful
> **break even** (idm) to earn only enough to pay expenses
> **component** (n) one of the parts of something
> **fluctuate** (v) to change frequently from one level to another
> **outweigh** (v) to be greater or more important than something else
> **proposition** (n) a proposal or suggestion, especially in business
> **revenue** (n) the money that a business receives regularly
> **transition** (n) a change from one state or condition to another

1 The price of oil has _____ dramatically since 2000, going from $40 a barrel to almost $150 then down to $30!

2 My friend came to me with an interesting business _____ , but I think it sounds a little too risky for me.

3 My daughter is a(n) _____ chef in New York. She hopes to get a job in a famous restaurant.

4 The benefits of this medication _____ its potential risks.

5 One _____ of the course focuses on reading comprehension and the other focuses on listening skills.

6 It can take teenagers a long time to make the _____ into adulthood.

7 The first year, our business lost money, the second year it _____ , and this year we made a profit.

8 Amazon's _____ in 2015 was over $100 billion ($100,000,000,000).

Scanning to preview a text

Scanning can be used to preview a text to determine whether it is worth reading fully. When you are doing research, it can help you find the texts that are most relevant to your topic. Scanning is especially useful when you are looking for specific information like names and numbers because those tend to stand out visually.

To scan, move your eyes quickly through the text with a search term in mind. Look for clues, for example, a capital letter (for names), a number or series of numbers (for amounts), or a symbol (dollar sign, quotation marks, percent sign, etc.).

3 Scan the article on page 92 to find the answers to these questions.

1 What are average start-up costs for a food truck? _____

2 What kind of mobile business did Rick Harper start? _____

3 What are some other examples of mobile retail?

_____

4 How much did mobile retail grow between 2009 and 2014?

_____

5 What are some of the problems that mobile retail owners face?

_____

6 How much money do food trucks bring in annually? _____

4 Scan the article again. Decide whether this article would be worth reading for each of these people. Write *Y* (yes), *N* (no), or *M* (maybe).

1 A small business owner who wants to find a bigger location _____

2 A small business owner who wants to expand into other parts of the city but isn't sure where _____

3 A person who wants to open a restaurant but doesn't have much money _____

4 A person looking for a job with a tech company _____

5 A researcher looking for current economic trends _____

6 A researcher looking for information on traffic flow in a city _____

WHILE READING

5 What is the writer's main argument? Write your answer in one sentence. Compare ideas with a partner.

_____

_____

_____

PRISM Digital Workbook

READING FOR
MAIN IDEAS

STARTING OUT MOBILE

1　Maybe you make the world's best peanut butter cookies, or you've always helped your friends and neighbors by fixing their computers, or perhaps you have a green thumb and your garden is the envy of the neighborhood. A lot of businesses are started by people who have hobbies or special talents and want to turn these interests into a business. But scaling up from a hobby to a real business, such as a bakery, restaurant, or store, requires business know-how and a substantial investment. Many entrepreneurs don't have enough of either of these, so they never take the first step.

2　An increasing number of **aspiring** business owners have found a way to take a first step that makes this **transition** from hobby to business more gradual, less expensive, and less risky. They are taking their dreams and talents on the road—in trucks. The first entrepreneurs to do this were in the food business. In recent years, a wave of food trucks have arrived on the scene, serving everything from gourmet muffins to empanadas to Korean tacos. Food trucks became a way for aspiring chefs to try out recipes and test the waters before making a big investment in a traditional, brick-and-mortar business[1].

3　Beginning on a small scale has its advantages, the most important of which is the relatively modest size of initial start-up costs. These costs, which consist primarily of the truck and any required equipment, usually come to about $20,000–$30,000, a fraction of what it would cost to start a store or restaurant. Similarly, overhead costs[2] are generally low. Mobile business owners must pay for gas, of course, but other utility payments are modest. With such tightly controlled costs, mobile businesses often **break even** in a year or two; in contrast, success comes to brick-and-mortar businesses much more slowly, and they often fail within the first two years. In short, mobile businesses are relatively low-risk **propositions**.

4　The success of food trucks inspired other entrepreneurs to consider starting out on wheels. Rich Harper once ran a chain of gyms, but his real interest was boxing. In 2005, he bought an old truck, equipped it with some gym equipment, and took to

the streets—all for a total start-up cost of $6,000. His business quickly turned a profit and is still going strong, as he brings the boxing ring to customers all over his state.

5　Today, there are trucks that sell flowers, shoes, clothes, and all kinds of specialty food items. There are also trucks that provide services, such as hair styling, dog grooming, and repair of high-tech devices. Mobile retail has grown steadily, posting a 12% increase between 2009 and 2014. Mobile retail is not without problems, however. Weather, the **fluctuating** price of gas, and just finding a place to park are all challenges that mobile entrepreneurs have to deal with every day. These business owners, however, feel the advantages **outweigh** the disadvantages. The mobile food business alone—the largest in the mobile retail sector—generates an average annual **revenue** of $857 million.

6　Once convinced that their business has achieved sufficient success, some successful mobile entrepreneurs move on to a brick-and-mortar business. Others, like Rich Harper and his boxing gym, are satisfied to stay mobile. In an interesting twist, some brick-and-mortar business owners, observing the success of mobile retailers, have added a mobile **component** to their business. The truck acts as a marketing tool to bring business into the store. As stand-alone businesses or as extensions of stores, mobile retail appears to be here to stay.

[1]**brick-and-mortar business** (n phr) a business with a physical location in a building
[2]**overhead costs** (n pl) expenses that come with the physical space of a business, such as property taxes and utility payments

READING BETWEEN THE LINES

WORKING OUT MEANING

6 Scan Reading 1 again to find these phrases. Use context to try to understand them. Then match them to the correct meaning.

1 (para 1) have a green thumb
2 (para 1) the envy of the neighborhood
3 (para 1) scale up
4 (para 2) arrive on the scene
5 (para 2) test the waters
6 (para 4) going strong
7 (para 6) move on to
8 (para 6) stand-alone

a try out in a safe way or on a small scale
b be good at growing plants
c become relatively common
d doing very well
e something your neighbors wish they had
f independent
g take to the next level
h exchange for (something different)

7 Work with a partner. Write a sentence for each phrase in Exercise 6, using the phrase in context correctly. Share your sentences with the class.

DISCUSSION

8 Work with a partner. Discuss the questions.

1 What role do you think social media plays in the rise of mobile retail?
2 In what way, if any, do you think the rise of mobile retail is related to the state of the economy?
3 Do you think mobile retail will continue to grow? Why or why not?

READING 2

PREPARING TO READ

USING YOUR KNOWLEDGE

1 You are going to read an article about customer loyalty. Check (✔) the strategies that would be successful in keeping you as a loyal customer. Then compare your choices with a partner. Discuss your reasons.

a Special prices for loyal customers ☐

b Free shipping ☐

c A program that rewards you for buying more merchandise ☐

d Special products for loyal customers ☐

e The opportunity to buy products in high demand before the general public ☐

f Prizes or gifts ☐

2 Read the sentences and choose the best definition for the words in bold.

1 When gasoline prices are low, drivers have no **incentive** to leave their cars at home and take public transportation.
   a alternative
   b encouragement
   c argument

2 Some investors **shrewdly** bought property when prices were very low.
   a based on good judgment
   b based on illegal actions
   c based on luck or coincidence

3 It is important to set goals that are **attainable**; otherwise, you will just get discouraged.
   a able to be reached
   b practical; sensible
   c simple; able to be explained clearly

4 There is an **ongoing** debate in this country about the role of education in economic success.
   a formal
   b highly emotional
   c continuing

5 We have lived in this house for more than thirty years, so we have **accumulated** a lot of possessions.
   a gradually collected
   b rid ourselves of
   c increased the value of

6 The university's student **retention** rate has improved in the past ten years—almost 80% of students who start here graduate from here.
   a academic performance
   b holding; keeping
   c quality or standards

7 He was a **pioneer** in bioengineering, publishing one of the earliest studies in the field.
   a one of the first people to do something
   b one of the most famous people in a field
   c an international expert

8 After one company started to offer free shipping to its customers, other companies soon **followed suit**.
   a made a more attractive offer
   b competed against one another
   c did the same thing

Keeping Your Customers

1   It costs five to ten times more to sell a product to a new customer than to an existing one. So what are businesses doing to hold on to their customers? The answer is—everything they possibly can. Two popular business strategies with successful track records for customer retention are rewards programs, often also referred to as loyalty programs, and subscription services.

2   Loyalty programs encourage customers to continue buying products or services from one particular company by offering customers rewards. Airlines, pioneers of loyalty programs, provide a good example. When customers fly with one airline on multiple trips, that airline rewards them with free travel. Generally, customers have to accumulate a specific number of "miles" or "points" in order to receive their reward, providing an incentive to continue flying with one airline. Other companies, from Starbucks to Best Buy, have followed suit, offering rewards to loyal customers.

3   American consumers often belong to multiple loyalty programs, yet most people participate actively in only a few. Companies are interested in understanding the reasons behind this behavior. The most successful loyalty programs have several features in common. They are simple and easy to understand, but most important, their rewards are attainable. Customers receive rewards often enough that they see the benefit of remaining loyal to the company. The programs not only keep customers buying the company's products or services, they also provide the company with valuable information about their customers' behavior and preferences.

4   A second successful strategy for maintaining customer relationships is the subscription service. In these programs customers sign up to purchase items, such as shaving products, snacks, or makeup, on a regular basis. These items are delivered to the customer's home. The convenience of home delivery is an idea with a long history, but subscription services offer more than a convenient way to replace household necessities. They offer customers products that are tailored to their own personal needs and desires. This kind of treatment makes customers feel special and deepens their connection to the brand. In a retail environment where consumers are faced with a dizzying array of products, this kind of service can combat what has been referred to as "the paralysis of choice." In other words, the service makes decisions for consumers who may have difficulty making decisions for themselves. For the company, subscription services offer guaranteed regular sales, an ongoing relationship with their customers, and, like loyalty programs, a rich source of data about buying behavior.

5   Some companies, such as Amazon, even charge their customers for their subscription service. In return, customers get what they value most, for example, free shipping or access to digital content. It may seem as if Amazon would lose money by not charging their customers for shipping, but the company has shrewdly calculated that customers, having paid for the subscription service, will shop on Amazon even for items they might otherwise buy at the local supermarket. One study showed that Amazon subscription customers spent an average of $1,500 per year, compared to non-subscription customers, who spent just $625.

6   Rewards programs and subscription services are just two of the marketing tools that businesses use to hold on to customers. They have learned that it makes better business sense to devote attention and even money to their current customers than to try to attract new ones.

WHILE READING

3 Read the article. Which of these statements are consistent with the claims made there? Compare your answers with a partner.

a Businesses are less concerned with keeping customers than with finding new ones. ☐

b Rewards programs are a good way to keep customers loyal. ☐

c Customers will not participate in loyalty programs if the goals are too hard to reach. ☐

d The main reason customers participate in subscription programs is the low price of joining them. ☐

e Subscription services are more successful than loyalty programs in attracting and keeping customers. ☐

f Subscription programs can increase sales. ☐

4 Scan the article to find the information to complete these paragraphs.

> The most effective loyalty programs are (1)_____ and have (2)_____ rewards. Keeping customers loyal is not the only reason for such programs. They also provide (3)_____ information about what (4)_____ like. (5)_____ were the first to offer rewards programs, and they are probably still the most familiar to the public.
>
> Subscription services offer more than (6)_____ ; they also offer products that are specific to customers' needs and (7)_____ . They offer a limited selection, which helps customers make (8)_____ . Research suggests that customers buy more products when they have a subscription. Amazon subscription members spend an average of (9)_____ per year, compared to non-subscription customers, who spend only about (10)_____ .

READING BETWEEN THE LINES

5 Work with a partner. Discuss the questions.

1 How do you think loyalty programs provide companies with data on customer behavior?

2 Why might customers join a loyalty program but then not participate actively in it?

3 What does the term *the paralysis of choice* mean?

4 Why might products such as snacks, razors for shaving, and makeup be popular items for subscription services?

DISCUSSION

6 Work with a partner. Use ideas from Reading 1 and Reading 2 to discuss the questions.

1 Do you participate in a loyalty program? If so, what do you like or not like about it? If not, why not?
2 Do you participate in a subscription service? If so, do you think having the subscription has encouraged you to buy more? If not, why not?
3 Why do you think it is so much easier to hold on to existing customers than to attract new ones?

⊙ LANGUAGE DEVELOPMENT

EXPRESSING CONTRAST

There are many different ways to signal that you are contrasting ideas. Contrast signals may differ in both structure and meaning.

Structure

Unlike other companies, Amazon charges for its subscription service.

Many subscription services are free; Amazon, **by contrast**, charges a substantial fee for its program.

Meaning

Contrast signals typically express one of three somewhat different meanings.

	prepositions	transition word or phrase
direct contrast	*unlike* *in contrast to*	*by contrast* *however* *on the other hand*
concession: to show that the contrast might not be complete or is unexpected	*despite* *in spite of*	*nevertheless* *yet* *however*
correction or replacement: to show that the first clause or phrase is wrong or insufficient and that the clause that follows is correct	*instead of* *rather than*	*instead* *on the contrary* *in fact* *rather* *however*

1 Read the sentences. Choose the best contrast signal. Pay attention to structure and meaning.

1 _____ the convenience of subscription services, these programs are not as popular as loyalty programs.

   a Instead of   **b** In spite of   **c** Nevertheless

2 One company has decided to avoid the whole point system in their loyalty program. _____ , they give their loyal customers their rewards immediately.

   a Instead   **b** However   **c** On the other hand

3 About a quarter of all new restaurants fail in their first year. _____ , hundreds of entrepreneurs open restaurants every year, hoping to beat the odds.

   a Rather   **b** Despite   **c** Nevertheless

4 _____ loyalty programs, subscription programs restrict membership to special customers, giving those customers the sense that they belong to an exclusive club.

   a Unlike   **b** Instead of   **c** However

5 Mobile businesses are not as risky as they seem; _____ , they are less likely to lose money than brick-and-mortar businesses.

   a by contrast   **b** in fact   **c** on the other hand

BUSINESS AND MARKETING VOCABULARY

2 Complete the information about business and marketing with the correct form of the words and phrases from the box.

> break even   brick-and-mortar   generate revenue
> marketing tool   on a large/small scale   start-up costs
> track record   turn a profit   utilities

    For many people, the dream of a lifetime is owning their own business. If you are one of them, it is a good idea to start (1)_____ . You may want to begin with a mobile business, where (2)_____ and (3)_____ are low. Whatever you decide, you should set goals for your new business. For example, how long do you expect it to take before your business (4)_____ ? How much longer after that will it take for the business to (5)_____ ?

    Even for an established (6)_____ business with a good (7)_____ , there comes a time when sales start to slow down, and you need to find a new way to (8)_____ . The question is, "What do your customers want?" There are lots of online (9)_____ that can help you learn more about your customers. So don't wait—start thinking about your marketing strategy today!

WRITING

CRITICAL THINKING

At the end of this unit, you are going to write a report that compares and contrasts different business models for a new venture or customer retention programs for an existing business. Look at this unit's Writing Task below.

Option A: Not all products and services fit the same business model. Some might have a more successful introduction in a mobile setting. For others, a mobile setting would not be appropriate. Compare and contrast two products or services regarding their potential as a mobile business.

Option B: Not all customer retention programs fit every type of business or product. Compare and contrast the appropriateness of loyalty programs and subscription services for a product or business that you have chosen.

1 Work in small groups. Why would new retail business owners decide to start their business in a mobile setting? List the advantages and disadvantages that are discussed in Reading 1 and your own ideas.

UNDERSTAND

advantages	disadvantages
lower risk	parking

2 With your group, complete the tasks.

EVALUATE

1 Review the list of potential new businesses below.
2 Decide whether each one would work better as a mobile or a traditional business. Give reasons for your choice.
3 Add one more idea of your own for a product or service that you think would make a good mobile business.

a yoga studio	health screening (simple blood tests, blood pressure, etc.)
a tanning salon	
vintage clothing	books
legal advice	art classes for children
organic fruit and vegetables	mobile phone and tablet repair
pizza	tax return preparation
T-shirts	_____

3 Work with your group. Imagine the management team at a business needs to decide whether to launch a loyalty program or a subscription service. For which kinds of products would each of these be appropriate? Fill in the chart with information from Reading 2 and your own ideas.

loyalty programs	subscription services
good for products that consumers buy often	good for products that consumers buy often

EVALUATE

4 With your group, complete the tasks.

1 Review the list of products.
2 Decide for which businesses a loyalty program would be more appropriate and for which a subscription service would be a better choice. Give reasons for your choice.
3 Add one more idea of your own for a business that you think would work well with either type of program.

> shoes
> school/office supplies
> coffee/tea
> gym/sports clothing
> health and beauty supplies (e.g., toothpaste)
> flowers
> music
> health food
> toys
> pet supplies
> high fashion clothing
> _____

REDUCTIONS OF SUBORDINATE CLAUSES

LANGUAGE

Subordinate clauses that contain the auxiliary verb *be* (that is, clauses that involve the progressive or passive) can be reduced to participial phrases when the subject of the two clauses is the same.

Reduction by deleting subject and auxiliary verb *be*

While **she was** surfing the Web, she discovered a new loyalty program.
  progressive subordinate clause

While surfing the Web, she discovered a new loyalty program.

Unless **they are** pushed by declining sales, some companies refuse to consider such tools.
  passive subordinate clause

Unless pushed by declining sales, some companies refuse to consider such tools.

Reduction by deleting subject, auxiliary verb *be*, and logical connector (*while, because, once, unless,* etc.)

Readers must infer the relationship between the two clauses. Sometimes, changes are needed to the main clause to preserve meaning.

While she was surfing the Web, she discovered a new loyalty program.
  progressive subordinate clause

Surfing the Web, she discovered a new loyalty program.

Unless they are pushed by declining sales, some companies refuse to consider such tools.
  passive subordinate clause

Pushed by declining sales, some companies **will finally consider** such tools.
                                          change to the main clause

Pushed by declining sales, these marketing tools can save a failing company.

PRISM **Digital** Workbook

1 Read the sentences. Underline the participial phrases and then rewrite them as full clauses. In some items, more than one answer is possible.

  1 Surprised by the rude behavior of the sales assistant, Karina never returned to the store.

  _____

  _____

  2 While working on a food truck, Kwan developed enough experience to start his own business.

  _____

  _____

3 Looking at the message board at the community center, Isabelle got an idea for a new mobile business—a dog-washing service at the park!

_____

_____

4 Once discovered by the food reporter for a local foodie site, the Tina's Tacos truck had more business than its owners could handle.

_____

_____

5 Encouraged by the good reviews of her friends, Alya joined a subscription program for natural beauty products.

_____

_____

2 Rewrite the sentences. Reduce the first clause to a participial phrase and make any other changes that may be necessary to preserve meaning. In some items, more than one answer is possible.

1 Claudia was hurt by the negative response to her cooking, so she decided not to open a restaurant.

_____

_____

_____

2 While he was researching marketing tools, David was surprised to learn about the inconsistent track record of loyalty programs.

_____

_____

_____

3 Unless they are embraced by a large number of customers, loyalty programs are not a very effective marketing tool.

_____

_____

_____

4 Because they were worried about start-up costs, the Hernández brothers decided to begin their business online.

_____

_____

_____

5 If this advice is taken seriously, it can dramatically improve a company's chances of success.

_____

_____

_____

ACADEMIC WRITING SKILLS

Writing about similarities and differences

In formal essays and reports, writers often compare or contrast people, things, or ideas in order to make an argument. There are two common ways to organize a text that includes comparison and/or contrast:

- **Block organization:** the writer discusses all the features (cost, appearance, size) of one thing, and then those same features of a second thing.
- **Point-by-point organization:** the writer compares one feature at a time, usually one feature per paragraph. Point-by-point organization works best when there are clear parallel points for comparison

1 Work with a partner. Complete the task.

PRISM Digital Workbook

1 Which organizational pattern does each outline represent?
Organizational pattern: _____

College A _____
Feature 1: _____
Feature 2: _____
Feature 3: _____

College B _____
Feature 1: _____
Feature 2: _____
Feature 3: _____

Organizational pattern: _____

Feature 1: _____
College A _____
College B _____

Feature 2: _____
College A _____
College B _____

Feature 3: _____
College A _____
College B _____

2 Think about the features of a college or university that can influence an applicant's choice. Choose three and fill in both outlines.

2 Read the very early draft of a student essay about the food truck industry. Then answer the questions with your partner.

Roy Choi is considered the pioneer of the modern food truck movement. He was born in South Korea but grew up in Los Angeles, surrounded by incredible diversity—including diverse food. He has worked in fancy restaurants and in food trucks. He was successful in both settings, but it was the dramatic and instant triumph of his first food truck, Kogi BBQ, that really shook up the food world. Choi says that working in each of the two settings taught him important lessons, allowing him to master both cooking and marketing.

Choi went to culinary school and then started working in hotel restaurants. What he learned in the theoretical world of culinary education did not prepare him for the real world of a busy hotel's kitchen (differences between what he was taught and the real world)

After years of classical cooking, he decided to make the switch to a smaller, less formal setting—a food truck. He wanted … (the advantages and disadvantages of the two settings and what he learned)

Conclusion

1 Which organizational pattern does this essay follow?
☐ **a** point-by-point organization
☐ **b** block organization

2 How could you reorganize the information to follow the other organizational pattern?

3 What would be the best conclusion for this essay? Give reasons for your choice.
a In conclusion, Choi was an important pioneer in the food truck business. Many people have followed Choi's success in this business.
b Today, the food truck business is an enormously successful industry, thanks, in part, to the initial popularity of Kogi BBQ and to the cooking and marketing skills Choi developed during his long career.
c Choi has been very successful. His experiences working in food trucks and in the kitchens of fine restaurants have both contributed to his achievements.
d Kogi BBQ has enjoyed enormous popularity. Choi's experience working in restaurants and food trucks may not be the only reason for his success, but it is certainly an important one.

WRITING TASK

PRISM Digital Workbook

Option A: Not all products and services fit the same business model. Some might have a more successful introduction in a mobile setting. For others, a mobile setting would not be appropriate. Compare and contrast two products or services regarding their potential as a mobile business.

Option B: Not all customer retention programs fit every type of business or product. Compare and contrast the appropriateness of loyalty programs and subscription services for a product or business that you have chosen.

PLAN

1 Decide on the structure of your report.

Step 1 Will you write Option A or Option B?

- If Option A, select two products or services from Critical Thinking, Exercise 2.
- If Option B, select one product from Critical Thinking, Exercise 4.

Step 2 What are the pros and cons? Use the ideas you discussed in the Critical Thinking activities. Use one of the following charts to organize your ideas:

- For Option A, list the advantages and disadvantages of a mobile setting for each of your products or services.

	pros of mobile setting	cons of mobile setting
product 1		
product 2		

- For Option B, list the advantages and disadvantages of a loyalty program and a subscription program for your product or service.

	pros for product	cons for product
loyalty program		
subscription program		

Step 3 Which organizational pattern is more appropriate for your report (see Academic Writing Skills, page 103)?
- block
- point-by-point

2 Refer to the Task Checklist on page 107 as you prepare your report.

WRITE A FIRST DRAFT

3 Write your compare and contrast report based on your plan. Write 500–600 words.

REVISE

4 Use the Task Checklist to review your report for content and structure.

TASK CHECKLIST	✔
Did you give some background information on mobile retail or customer retention programs?	
Does each paragraph include a topic sentence?	
Have you used an appropriate organizational structure for comparison and contrast?	
Have you provided evidence to support your argument in your body paragraphs?	
Does your concluding paragraph make recommendations or refer to considerations for the future?	

5 Make any necessary changes to your report.

EDIT

6 Use the Language Checklist to edit your report for language errors.

LANGUAGE CHECKLIST	✔
Have you chosen appropriate contrast markers for your intended meaning?	
Are your contrast markers structured correctly in terms of grammar?	
Have you used business and marketing vocabulary correctly? Did you hyphenate the terms correctly?	
Have you reduced some subordinate clauses with *be* to participial phrases, for sentence variety?	
Have you used the appropriate logical connectors for progressive and passive clauses?	

7 Make any necessary changes to your report.

ON CAMPUS

PRIORITIZING YOUR TIME

A typical week at college is busy and hectic. Successful students find it helpful to take the time to organize their week's activities and prioritize all of the tasks they need to do according to importance and due dates.

PREPARING TO READ

1 Work with a partner. Discuss the questions.

1 Do you establish goals on a weekly basis? What's an example of a goal you have for this week?
2 If you have just an hour of free time between classes, how do you use that time?
3 How do you deal with invitations from friends when you have a lot to do?

WHILE READING

2 Read the flyer on the next page from an Academic Support Center about prioritizing time. Then read these statements. Write *G* (good strategy) or *B* (bad strategy).

1 Write specific details for each task. _____
2 Do the easy tasks first. _____
3 Revise and remove items from the low-priority list if necessary. _____
4 Do high-priority tasks when you have more time. _____
5 Label all social activities as low priority. _____
6 Reschedule high-priority tasks into next week if they don't get finished. _____

PRACTICE

3 Work with a partner. Discuss the priority levels of this student's tasks and label them *L* (low priority), *M* (middle), or *H* (high). Share your ideas with another pair and explain your reasoning.

1 update social media site _____
2 send thank-you note to professor for reviewing an application _____
3 join International Student Association pizza party _____
4 write blog post about my new favorite restaurants near campus _____
5 research airline prices for Study Abroad trip _____
6 ask Professor Adams for a letter of recommendation _____

Students who organize their coursework and prioritize tasks usually do better than students who don't. Here are some simple steps to help you prioritize your time by making a weekly plan.

(1) STEP 1: LIST ALL YOUR TASKS FOR THE WEEK
- Be specific about what you need to do and by when. Instead of writing *read history*, write *history: read pp143–178 for Thursday's class.*
- Divide the list into academic tasks and personal tasks.

(2) STEP 2: PRIORITIZE YOUR TASKS
Label each task on your list as high, middle, or low priority.
- High priority: tasks necessary for this week, like studying for an upcoming test or going to a friend's wedding.
- Middle priority: tasks that need to be done but not necessarily this week, such as getting a scholarship application done early.
- Low priority: tasks you want to complete but which are not necessary, like attending a football game or doing an extra credit[1] project for class.

(3) STEP 3: MAKE A PLAN FOR THE WEEK
- Put high-priority tasks first on your daily schedule. When you have just a little time, do the easy middle- or low-priority tasks, like responding to personal email.
- During the week, review and revise the list. Don't be afraid to reschedule middle-priority tasks and remove low-priority tasks that you don't have time for.

COMMON MISTAKES TO AVOID:
- doing easy tasks first, not the most important ones
- rescheduling high-priority tasks until they become urgent[2] tasks
- panicking because everything feels high priority
- agreeing to do other things (like go out with friends) when high-priority tasks are waiting.

[1]**extra credit** (n) optional classwork that can improve a student's grade
[2]**urgent** (adj) very important; requiring immediate attention

REAL-WORLD APPLICATION

4 With your partner, create a plan for each of you for next week using the steps in the reading.

LEARNING OBJECTIVES

Reading skills	Use graphic organizers to take notes; interpret quotes
Grammar	Complex noun phrases with *what*
Academic writing skills	Cite quoted material; write an explanatory synthesis
Writing Task	Write an explanatory synthesis essay
On Campus	Managing high volumes of reading

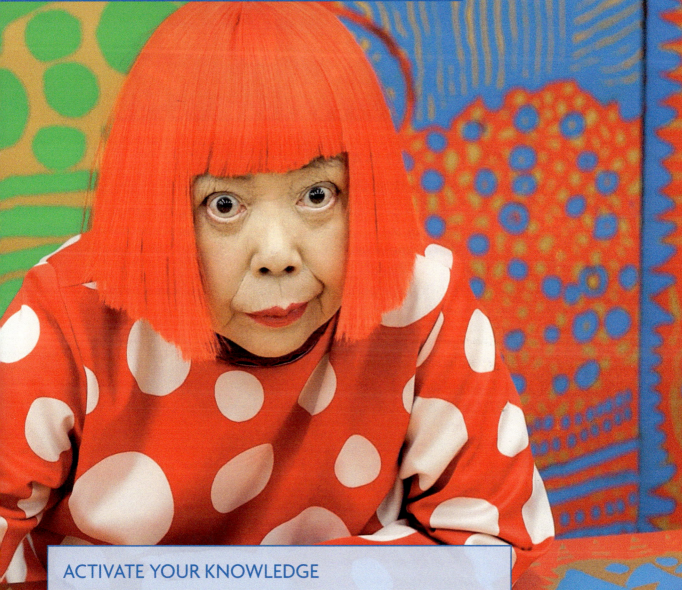

ACTIVATE YOUR KNOWLEDGE

Work with a partner. Discuss the questions.

1   Who is the person in the photo? What do you know about her?

2   Do you consider yourself a creative person? Why or why not?
    What does it mean to be creative?

3   Name three famous people, living or dead, whom you consider to
    be creative geniuses. In what ways are such people different from
    the rest of the population? What do they have that most people
    don't? Explain your answer.

PREPARING TO WATCH

ACTIVATING YOUR KNOWLEDGE

1 Work with a partner. Discuss the questions.

1 Do you think people are born creative or is creativity learned? Why do you think so?

2 What are some ways creativity can be encouraged? What are some ways it is inhibited?

3 Is creativity an important factor in your choice of career? Why or why not?

2 Check (✔) the statements you agree with. Discuss your answers with a partner.

1 All children are creative. ☐

2 Creativity is a talent, like playing the piano well or being good with numbers. ☐

3 Many occupations require creativity. ☐

4 Other people influence how creative we think we are. ☐

5 Creativity can be fostered and developed. ☐

GLOSSARY

breakthrough idea (n phr) an important or novel idea that helps to improve a situation or provide an answer to a problem

opt out (phr v) to choose not to be part of an activity or to stop being involved in it

foster (v) to encourage the development or growth of something

curator (n) a person in charge of a department of a museum or other place where objects of art, science, or from the past are collected, or a person who organizes and arranges a showing of art or other objects of interest

empathy (n) the ability to share someone else's feelings or experiences by imagining what it would be like to be in that person's situation

---

WHILE WATCHING

3 ▶ Watch the video. Circle the correct answer.

UNDERSTANDING MAIN IDEAS

1 What is creative confidence?
   a following new ideas without the fear of being judged
   b being brave enough to pursue your own innovative ideas
   c understanding your own particular kind of creativity

2 Why do many people stop believing they are creative?
   a They do not like being judged as creative or not.
   b A teacher told them that they are not very creative.
   c They are not good at drawing.

3 According to David Kelley, what is the real key to developing creativity?
   a understanding the needs of the people you want to create for
   b exploring the ideas of those in the technology and business fields
   c determining why something is meaningful to you

4 ▶ Watch the video again. Then complete the summary with one or two words in each space.

SUMMARIZING

The Kelley brothers have used their creativity to _____ many everyday objects. Their book, *Creative Confidence*, has been helping many people develop and foster their own creativity. While interviewing 100 people, they _____ that people have ideas, they just hold those ideas in. Being told that you are not creative has resulted in people _____ . Creativity needs to be _____ , just like playing the piano. People can enhance their creativity by building _____ for people. Once this happens, _____ ideas can emerge.

5 Work with a partner. Discuss the questions.

MAKING INFERENCES

1 Do you think the Kelley brothers were encouraged to be creative when they were young? Why or why not?

2 Who do you think they interviewed for their book?

3 Why do you think talking to people who use a particular product helps foster creativity in the redesign of that product?

DISCUSSION

6 Discuss the questions with your partner.

1 How have other people affected your creative confidence?

2 How can courage be fostered in young people?

3 Do you agree that empathy is the key to creativity? Why or why not?

4 Can empathy be fostered in young people? If so, how? If not, why not?

READING

PREPARING TO READ

UNDERSTANDING KEY VOCABULARY

1 You are going to read an article about mental illness and creativity. Read the definitions. Complete the sentences with the correct form of the words in bold.

> **intriguing** (adj) very interesting; mysterious
> **label** (v) to assign a (usually negative) characteristic to someone or something
> **norm** (n) accepted standard or way of doing something
> **notion** (n) idea
> **pursue** (v) to try to do something over a period of time
> **reject** (v) to refuse to accept
> **skeptical** (adj) doubting that something is true
> **suppress** (v) to prevent something from being expressed or known

1 She tried to _____ all her other thoughts in order to concentrate completely on the exam questions.

2 This kind of behavior is definitely not the _____ for animals that live in the wild, but an animal's behavior often changes when it lives in a zoo.

3 Most people are _____ of the stories about a monster that lives in the lake.

4 In spite of the substantial proof that our climate is getting warmer, some people still _____ the idea.

5 The _____ that the Earth is round actually goes back as far as 8,000 years ago.

6 The results of this study on creative thinking are _____ , but more research will be required to confirm them.

7 If you always complain and don't work well with others, you will be _____ as an unsatisfactory employee.

8 She's majoring in biology because she wants to _____ a career in medical research and neuroscience.

2 Read the first sentence of each paragraph of the article on page 116. Then check (✔) the topics you think will be discussed in the article. Compare answers with a partner.

    a the history of the connection between mental illness and creativity ☐

    b the causes of certain types of mental illness ☐

    c different points of view on the connection between mental illness and creativity ☐

    d how psychologists test people to determine if they are suffering from mental illness ☐

    e results of research studies on the connection between mental illness and creativity ☐

    f how experts define both creativity and mental illness ☐

3 Read the article and check your predictions.

WHILE READING

Using graphic organizers to take notes

Using a graphic organizer in your notes can help you understand and remember how ideas and facts are related.

4 Read the article again. Fill in the chart with information that supports the two sides of the issue presented in the article. Then compare your notes with a partner.

Connection between mental illness and creativity

yes	no
1970s study found 80% of subjects had mood disorders	most creative people are not mentally ill

Mental Illness and Creative Genius: Is There a Connection?

1   The association of mental illness with creative genius goes back to ancient times. The Greeks considered creative but troubled geniuses to be "touched by the gods." The list of tortured[1] artists throughout history is both long and familiar. It includes writers such as Hemingway, Tolstoy, and Woolf, painters, such as Gauguin, Van Gogh, and Kahlo, and musicians such as Mozart, Billie Holiday, and Kurt Cobain, to name just a few. Some artists report their own mental illness as crucial to their creative process while others curse their struggles. Van Gogh, in a letter to his brother, writes, "Oh, if I could have worked without this accursed disease— what things I might have done."

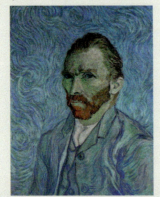

Van Gogh self-portrait (1889)

2   The scientific community is divided on what role, if any, mental illness plays in creativity. Several important early studies tried to establish this link. In the 1970s, neuroscientist Nancy Andreasen conducted a study of 30 well-known writers and found that 80% of them had experienced a major episode of mood disorder[2], compared with 30% of her control group. A subsequent study of 47 famous British writers and artists reported a lower, but still significant percentage reporting mood disorders.

3   These early studies were on a small scale and relied on interviews and self-reported behavior. More recent studies have been much larger and more scientifically rigorous[3]. In these studies, the connection found between creativity and mental illness has been weaker, yet, the authors argue, still important and worth **pursuing**. These studies suggest a genetic basis for both creativity and some forms of mental illness, pointing to a possible connection. Commenting on one of the largest studies, neurologist Dr. Kari Stefansson observed in a 2015 interview in *The Guardian*, "Often, when people are creating something new, they end up straddling … sanity and insanity."

4   Nevertheless, other members of the scientific community are **skeptical** of the association between creativity and mental illness, calling this a romantic, 19th-century **notion**. They stress the fact that most mentally ill individuals are not particularly creative, and most creative artists are in good mental health. Furthermore, they point out that creative artists who do suffer from mental illness usually work more effectively when their conditions are treated and controlled. They argue that any connection between mental illness and creativity may be the result of purely practical factors. People who don't fit in with societal **norms** and tend to think and act differently, perhaps even enough to be **labeled** mentally ill, may be attracted to a life in the arts, where their behavior is more likely to be accepted, or at least tolerated.

5   Still, even those who **reject** the notion of any direct or causal connection admit that creative artists and those who suffer from some forms of mental illness may share some characteristics. One recent study that compared these two groups revealed an **intriguing** result. Both populations showed high measures of one specific type of behavior: the inability to **suppress** competing stimuli and cognitive activity while focusing on a central task. In other words, they had difficulty performing the assigned task— remembering sequences of numbers—when they were presented with other information on a screen at the same time. They could not stop themselves from paying attention to this additional information. In 2013, psychologist Barry Kaufman, writing in a blog in the journal *Scientific American*, summarizes the study's findings this way, "It seems that the key to creative cognition is opening up the floodgates and letting in as much information as possible. Because you never know: sometimes the most bizarre associations can turn into the most productively creative ideas."

6   As the results of studies like these emerge, the scientific community will continue to debate the connection between mental health and creative thinking. In the public imagination, however, the notion persists that the creative genius straddles sanity and insanity.

[1]**tortured** (adj) deeply troubled
[2]**mood disorder** (n phr) psychological problems that involve extreme emotions
[3]**rigorous** (adj) strict; of a high standard

READING BETWEEN THE LINES

SKILLS

Interpreting quotes

Writers often include quotations from other people, especially experts. This allows writers to add another voice in support of their perspective. It is important for readers to interpret these quotations—understand what they mean and think about why they're relevant to the text—because they often contain key ideas.

MAKING INFERENCES

PRISM Digital Workbook

5 Work with a partner. Read each quotation and write your interpretation. Why do you think the writer included this quote in the text? Read the article again for context, if needed. Look up any words you don't know, especially the words in bold.

source	quote	your interpretation
Stefansson	"... when people are creating something new, they end up **straddling** ... sanity and insanity." (paragraph 3)	
Kaufman	"... the key to creative cognition is opening up the **floodgates** and letting in as much information as possible." (paragraph 5)	

6 Work with a partner. Complete the task.

The article describes a study in which participants had to do two things at once. Try a similar task:

- Count backwards from 1,000 by twos (1,000, 998, 996, 994, ...) while watching a video.
- Have your partner keep track of your progress.
- Switch roles and repeat the task.

1 How difficult was the task for each of you?
2 How could the ability to pay attention to two tasks at the same time be relevant to creativity? To mental illness?

DISCUSSION

7 Join another pair to form a small group. Discuss the questions.

1 Why do you think people with psychological problems are more likely to be tolerated in a community of artists?
2 What do you think is the source of creativity? Can it be taught or learned?
3 Do you know of someone who has psychological problems and who is also very creative? Describe this person.

READING 2

PREPARING TO READ

PREDICTING CONTENT USING VISUALS

1 You are going to read an article about creativity. Work in small groups. Complete the task. How do you think this task relates to creativity?

Imagine that you have only these items: a candle, a box of matches, and some thumbtacks.

Using only these items, how would you attach the candle to the wall so that the melting wax will not drip onto anything below it? (answer on page 131)

2 Read the sentences and choose the best definition for the words in bold.

1 I'm such a **procrastinator**. Whenever I have to write a paper, I always end up finishing it just hours before the deadline.

  a a person who worries a lot
  b a person who always makes excuses for mistakes
  c a person who waits as long as possible to begin work

2 The students receive a lot of intellectual **stimulation** at this school. They are encouraged to explore their world and try new things.

  a things that arouse interest
  b educational opportunity and activity
  c help with difficult things

3 The government is **seeking** new ways to create more employment opportunities.

  a starting to develop
  b gathering information about
  c trying to find

4 The speaker's words **triggered** an angry reaction from the crowd.

  a caused
  b described
  c softened

5 A government spokesman **confirmed** that two people had been hurt in the attack.

  a reported a suspicion
  b stated that something is true
  c denied that something is true

6 Engineers often have to be very **resourceful**, using whatever is available to solve problems.

  a skilled at solving problems
  b skilled at saving time, money, and energy
  c able to understand complex problems quickly

7 Scientists announced that they had made a **breakthrough** in their understanding of the development of cancer cells.

  a important discovery
  b research tool
  c new way of describing something

8 He decided to use an **innovative** approach to teaching science because more traditional approaches had been ineffective.

  a based on research
  b highly structured
  c new and different

The Creative Mind

1   What is the secret to the world's most creative minds—the minds of **resourceful** inventors, **innovative** scientists, and inspired artists? Such individuals are certainly intelligent, but intelligence cannot be the key, as numerous studies have shown that a high IQ alone does not lead to creativity. Creative thinkers seem to have a special way of thinking. Creativity researcher and neuroscientist Nancy Andreasen, in a 2014 *Atlantic Magazine* article, describes creative people as "better at recognizing relationships, making associations and connections, and seeing things in an original way—seeing things that others cannot see." For example, in the early 2000s, Jack Dorsey, one of the founders of Twitter, tried to use text alerts to improve the system for reserving and sending out taxis. He made a connection between two seemingly unrelated systems, but he was too far ahead of his time—the necessary technology was not yet available. Today, most taxi services use a version of Dorsey's original idea.

2   So what are the requirements for creativity? Psychologists contend that there are actually two levels of creative thinking which they refer to as "Big C" and "small c." Big C creativity applies to **breakthrough** ideas, ones that may change the course of a field or even history. Small c creativity refers to everyday creative problem solving, which psychologists subdivide further into convergent and divergent thinking. Convergent thinking involves examining all of the facts and arriving at a single solution. In contrast, divergent thinking involves coming up with many possible solutions, for example, thinking of many different uses for a brick or paper clip. What most people think of as creativity generally involves divergent thinking.

3   Andreasen and others investigating the sources of creativity have noted that small c creativity does not always lead to Big C breakthroughs. True creative geniuses seem to have additional characteristics, ones that do not always fit in well with societal norms. These people seem wired[1] to **seek** novelty, take risks, and push limits in their explorations. The reward centers in their brains seem to need more than the average amount of **stimulation** in order to release dopamine, the chemical that **triggers** feelings of pleasure. As children, they were often unable to sit still, unable to focus on their lessons, instead, always looking for something new and interesting to capture their attention. Today, children who display this kind of behavior are often labeled ADHD[2] because they cause problems in the classroom. These same characteristics were probably extremely useful in the past—when humans depended on hunting, a risky and unpredictable but exciting activity—and researchers suspect they may also contribute to creativity.

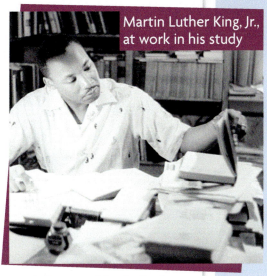

Martin Luther King, Jr., at work in his study

4   Creativity, with a big or small c, takes time. We tend to think of breakthroughs as coming in a sudden flash of genius, but this is rarely the case. Ideas often evolve and form over a long period. Andreasen, referring to her study of creative thinking, described her findings this way, "… almost all of my subjects confirmed that when eureka moments³ occur, they tend to be precipitated by long periods of preparation and incubation⁴, and to strike when the mind is relaxed." In fact, many of history's most creative people have a reputation as procrastinators. Martin Luther King, Jr., reportedly wrote his "I Have a Dream" speech at ten o'clock the night before he delivered it, though it had mostly likely gone through a long period of "preparation and incubation" in his mind before that.

5   The search for the source of creativity continues. Most researchers agree that the answer will be complex and that there is probably no single characteristic, no single secret to explain the world's most creative minds.

¹**wired** (adj) biologically programmed
²**ADHD** (n) Attention Deficit Hyperactivity Disorder
³**eureka moment** (idm) the point at which you suddenly understand the answer or solution to a problem
⁴**incubation** (n) protected development

WHILE READING

3 Read the article. Write *M* (main idea), *D* (detail), or *X* (information not given) next to the statements.

1 Creative people have a special way of thinking. _____
2 Andreasen's research explores the connection between intelligence and creativity. _____
3 Divergent thinking means finding many different ways to solve a problem. _____
4 Creative thinkers seek new experiences. _____
5 The painter Van Gogh was known to take a lot of risks. _____
6 Some aspects of creative behavior may have been beneficial to early humans. _____
7 Creative thinking is often a slow process. _____
8 Many creative people also procrastinate. _____

4 Read the article again. Take notes about creativity by filling in details in this graphic organizer.

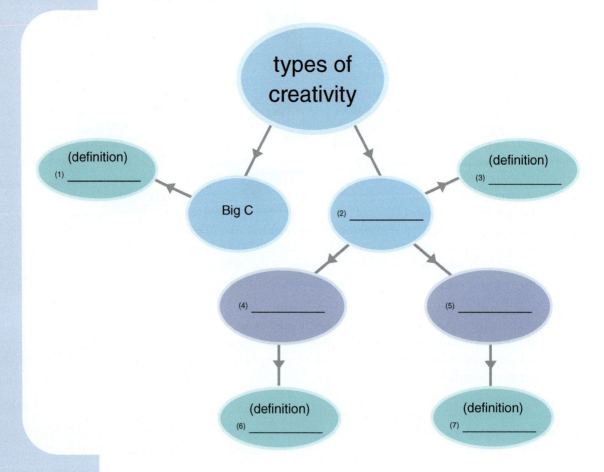

READING BETWEEN THE LINES

5 Work in small groups. Discuss the questions.

1 How does the example of Jack Dorsey illustrate creativity?
2 How is procrastination related to the concept of incubation?
3 Why might an early human with ADHD have been a good hunter?

DISCUSSION

6 With your group, use your notes from Reading 1 and Reading 2 to discuss the questions.

1 Are you more of a convergent or divergent thinker? Why?
2 What different kinds of tasks or professions are more appropriate for convergent thinkers? For divergent thinkers? Why?
3 Think of a behavior that used to be acceptable but is now labeled abnormal, or even a sign of mental illness. Why do you think it was acceptable in the past but not now?

EXPERIMENTAL SCIENCE TERMINOLOGY

Read the summary of a child development study. Write the words and phrases in bold next to their definitions below.

PRISM **Digital** Workbook

> A study that began in 1986 **established a causal link** between the behavior of parents and the success of their children. The **research subjects** in this study were the families of 129 children living in poverty in Jamaica. There were two **experimental groups**, and each group received a different treatment. In one, the children received extra food and milk. In the other, the families received visits from an expert in early childhood development, who encouraged the parents to spend more time engaged with their children: reading books, singing songs, or simply playing. A third set of families, the **control group**, received no treatment. The experiment lasted for two years, but the researchers who **conducted the study** continued to follow the children.
>
> The researchers found that the **intervention** that made the most difference in the children's lives was early parental interaction. As they were growing up, the children in this group exhibited more positive behavior and had higher IQ scores than the children in the other groups. As adults, they earn 25% more than the other participants in the study. The researchers **contend** that their results have clear **implications**. To ensure the future success of children living in poverty, educate parents about the importance of parent–child interaction.

1 _____ (v phr) to do academic research, such as an experiment

2 _____ (n) action taken to deal with a problem

3 _____ (n) conclusions suggested by the results of an academic study

4 _____ (n phr) participants in an experiment who do not receive experimental treatment

5 _____ (n phr) participants in an experiment who receive experimental treatment

6 _____ (n) all the participants in an experiment

7 _____ (v phr) to show a cause-and-effect connection

8 _____ (v) to claim

WRITING

CRITICAL THINKING

At the end of this unit, you are going to write an explanatory synthesis essay in which you synthesize information from different sources but do not make an argument of your own. Look at this unit's Writing Task below.

> What is creative thinking? Explain the current understanding of this concept, synthesizing information from different sources.

ANALYZE

1 Read Reading 1 and Reading 2 again. As you read, make annotations in the margins that sum up in a few words the topics that are discussed and the main points the writer is making about them. Compare your annotations with a partner.

(annotation) history of connection betw. creativity & ment ills

1   The association of mental illness with creative genius goes back to ancient times. The Greeks considered creative but troubled geniuses to be "touched by the gods." The list of tortured artists throughout history is both long and familiar. It includes writers such as Hemingway, Tolstoy, and Woolf, painters, such as Gauguin, Van Gogh, and Kahlo, and musicians such as Mozart, Billie Holiday, and Kurt Cobain, to name just a few. Some artists report their own mental illness as crucial to their creative process while others curse their struggles. Van Gogh, in a letter to his brother, writes, "Oh, if I could have worked without this accursed disease— what things I might have done."

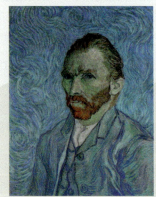
Van Gogh self-portrait (1889)

2 Use your notes to complete this chart. Check (✔) the topics that are discussed in each article. Add any other topics that you think are important. (If you have done outside research, annotate those sources and add them to your chart.) Compare your chart with those of your classmates.

▲ APPLY

	Reading 1	Reading 2
a historical background	✔	
b definitions or explanations of concepts		
c research findings		
d descriptions of creative behavior		
e specific examples of the accomplishments of creative individuals		
f advantages and disadvantages of creativity		

3 Work with a partner. Write one or two sentences that sum up what you have learned about creativity in this unit. Consider all of the material you have read as well as your notes.

CREATE ▲

_____

_____

_____

_____

_____

_____

GRAMMAR FOR WRITING

COMPLEX NOUN PHRASES WITH *WHAT*

A complex noun phrase with *what* can perform the same function as a noun + relative clause.

In a complex noun phrase beginning with *what*, the pronoun *what* replaces both the relative pronoun and the noun (phrase) it refers to. However, *what* can only be used to replace general terms like "the things/stuff/activities that ..."

These complex noun phrases can appear as subjects or objects. Notice that, although "the things/stuff/activities" are plural, *what* always takes a singular verb.

Subject: **What most people think of as creativity** generally involves divergent thinking.

Object: The quiet environment and free time gave him exactly **what he needed** in order to think creatively.

Complex noun phrases with *what* add variety to a writer's sentences. This structure is also an efficient and elegant way to draw attention to a point.

PRISM | Digital Workbook

1 Rewrite the sentences so that they contain a complex noun phrase with *what*. Make sure to use the correct verb form after *what*.

1 The articles describe the activities that the research subjects in the study did in order to demonstrate their creativity.

_____

_____

2 The things that have long been considered signs of mental illness may actually be part of the creative process.

_____

_____

3 We still don't know for certain the things that lead to creativity.

_____

_____

4 The researchers were looking for the things that single out the most creative people in the population.

_____

_____

5 One of the goals of the study was to find out the activities that creative people are doing when they come up with their best ideas.

_____

_____

2 Write three sentences of your own about creativity using complex noun phrases with *what*.

1 _____

_____

2 _____

_____

3 _____

_____

ACADEMIC WRITING SKILLS

CITING QUOTED MATERIAL

Using a variety of sentence types can be particularly useful in summaries and syntheses when you want to distance your own writing from the original text.

You can increase variety by changing the length, type, order, and pattern of sentences you use. You can also add variety by using direct quotations, which can provide interesting details and important support in an essay.

When you use someone's exact words, make sure you use quotation marks and cite the source of the quotation. The source may include the person's name as well as when and where the words appeared.

In an interview with the World Bank in **2015**, one of the authors of the 1986 Jamaica study, **Elaine Burke**, explained, "Because of this, even before we could stimulate the children, we had to stimulate the parents and get them to understand the importance of toys and appropriate language."

1 Scan Reading 1 and Reading 2 to find the quotations attributed to each of these experts and the source information. Then write a sentence of your own citing the quotation.

PRISM Digital Workbook

1 Kari Stefansson (Reading 1)

Year: _____ Source: _____

_____

_____

_____

2 Nancy Andreasen (Reading 2)

Year: _____ Source: _____

_____

_____

_____

2 Do some research to find two or three more quotes about creativity or creative thinking that you could cite in your essay.

1 Quote: _____

_____

_____

Year: _____   Source: _____

2 Quote: _____

_____

_____

Year: _____   Source: _____

3 Quote: _____

_____

_____

Year: _____   Source: _____

WRITING AN EXPLANATORY SYNTHESIS

An explanatory synthesis is similar to a summary in that it directly reports the content of another source. As in a summary, you choose the most important information in the source texts and paraphrase it. In a synthesis, however, you must weave the information in the sources together to make a coherent new text.

Because you are reporting the work of other writers, you will not make a claim based on your own views. However, you will still need a thesis statement to give your readers an idea about the content of your essay.

As you prepare to write your essay, a simple T-chart can help you gather and organize your ideas.

3 Make a T-chart to gather and organize your ideas. See the example T-chart in Exercise 6 on the next page.

4 Look back at the table of topics in Critical Thinking, Exercise 2. Choose three or four that you think are most important for describing our current understanding of creativity. Write them in your T-chart. Be sure to include some topics that are discussed in more than one source.

5 Review your annotations in the margins of Reading 1 and Reading 2 (and any other sources you are using). Use your annotations to make notes on each of the topics in your T-chart. Be sure to use your own words—doing so now will make it easier to write your synthesis later (and avoid any suggestion of plagiarism).

6 For each topic, use your notes to write one or two sentences that bring together (synthesize) the ideas from all sources. These will be your topic sentences. Write them in another column.

topic	notes	topic sentences
creative behavior	R1: being open to all input & possibilities, coming up with new & interesting connections btw ideas	Creative thinkers see unexpected connections between ideas and find a range of ways to approach a problem or task. In doing so, they often push limits and take risks.
	Kaufman quote	
	R2: Recognizing connections, coming up with different solutions	
	Dorsey example, def of divergent thinking, search for novelty, risk	

WRITING TASK

What is creative thinking? Explain the current understanding of this concept, synthesizing information from different sources.

PRISM **Digital** Workbook

PLAN

1 Think about your introductory paragraph.

1 Review the sentences you wrote in Critical Thinking, Exercise 3. Use the ideas in those sentences to write a thesis statement about our current understanding of creativity. (Remember, in an explanatory synthesis essay, you will not state and defend an argument based on your own views.)

_____

_____

_____

2 Look again at the chart in Critical Thinking, Exercise 2. Which topics could or should appear in your introductory paragraph?

2 Think about your body paragraphs.

1 Decide on the order of your points.
First body paragraph: _____
Second body paragraph: _____
Third body paragraph: _____

2 You have already written your topic sentences (Academic Writing Skills, Exercise 6). What other details do you want to include in each paragraph to support the ideas you expressed in the topic sentences? Review the notes in your T-chart and your annotations, and, if you need to, review the articles themselves.

3 What quotation(s) from Reading 1, Reading 2, or other sources would be appropriate to cite in your explanatory synthesis essay?

3 Think about your conclusion. What thoughts do you want to leave your readers with?

4 Refer to the Task Checklist as you prepare your essay.

WRITE A FIRST DRAFT

5 Write your explanatory synthesis essay based on your essay plan. Write 500–600 words.

REVISE

6 Use the Task Checklist to review your essay for content and structure.

TASK CHECKLIST	✔
Have you introduced and explained your topic?	
Have you included information from all your sources?	
Have you paraphrased the information in the articles in your own words?	
Have you used quotations from experts?	
Have you used a variety of sentence structures?	
Does your concluding paragraph leave your readers with something to think about?	

7 Make any necessary changes to your essay.

EDIT

8 Use the Language Checklist to edit your essay for language errors.

LANGUAGE CHECKLIST	✔
Did you use terminology from experimental science correctly?	
Did you draw attention to a point by using a complex noun phrase with *what*?	
Did you cite the source and year of any quotations properly?	
Did you punctuate quotations accurately?	

9 Make any necessary changes to your essay.

Answer to the puzzle on page 118:

ON CAMPUS

MANAGING HIGH VOLUMES OF READING

SKILLS One of the biggest shocks for many new college students is the amount of reading they have to do. There are ways to manage the workload, but it takes practice.

PREPARING TO READ

1 Work with a partner. What strategies for managing reading volume do you predict will be presented? Come back to check your predictions after you read the text.

_____   _____   _____

WHILE READING

2 Read the comments on the next page from an Academic Support Center discussion board thread about how to deal with a high volume of reading. Write *T* (true) or *F* (false).

_____ 1 Students should read every word of an assigned text.

_____ 2 You read differently for a class discussion than for a test.

_____ 3 It is good to read before you go to sleep because you are relaxed.

_____ 4 It can take some time to become good at the suggested strategies.

_____ 5 You can usually understand the main idea of a chapter by previewing it.

_____ 6 It is helpful to read the study questions in a textbook before doing the reading.

PRACTICE

3 Work with a partner. Discuss the questions.

1 Which strategies from the discussion board would be easiest for you to implement?

2 Which strategies from the discussion board would be most difficult for you to implement?

I love to read, so I'm surprised that I'm finding it so difficult to keep up with all the assigned reading at college. Does anyone have any suggestions for me?

Jill Graham, freshman, undeclared[1]

Ask yourself why you are reading this particular text. That will tell you what you should focus on. A class discussion? Read for main ideas (arguments, causes, effects, etc). A paper? Read for data and ideas that support your topic. A test? Read for detail with a focus on information that has been mentioned in lectures.

Peter Edmonds, Academic Support Center

A lot of students just dive into a text without really knowing anything about it. Take three minutes and look through the reading. Notice the name of the chapter (not just "Chapter 3"), the headings, subheadings, photos, captions, graphs, and charts. These will give you some context and help you take in the information better.

Melanie Cutler, Academic Support Center

My students tell me all the time that they didn't realize there is a glossary in the back of the book, or that there were discussion questions in the chapters. When you get a textbook, spend some time with it. Look at the table of contents, understand how the chapters are organized, read the preface[2], and look at material in the back of the book.

Janice Walker, professor of anthropology and textbook writer

You can't read everything in depth[3]. It's just too much. I read the introduction and conclusion or summary at the end. If there are study questions, I read those. Then I can decide if it's worth my time to read more carefully. You just need to prioritize.

Pedro Gonzales, Business Administration

I skim until I come to something that seems important, and then I read that section more carefully. I look for signal words and phrases like *cause, effect, conclusion, on the other hand, There are three key reasons* …. I also pay attention to lists.

Gülcin San, senior, Sociology

These are all great ideas, but they take time and practice. My quick and easy strategy is this: Read when you have the most energy. For me, that's the morning. Avoid bedtime reading. And don't think you can stay up all night to finish the reading. It won't stick if you're tired.

Brendan Richards, Library Science

---

[1]**undeclared** (adj) undecided about a major
[2]**preface** (n) introduction to a book that explains its purpose
[3]**in depth** (adv) carefully and completely

REAL-WORLD APPLICATION

4 Write a response to Jill Graham with the best advice you have for managing workload. Share your ideas in small groups.

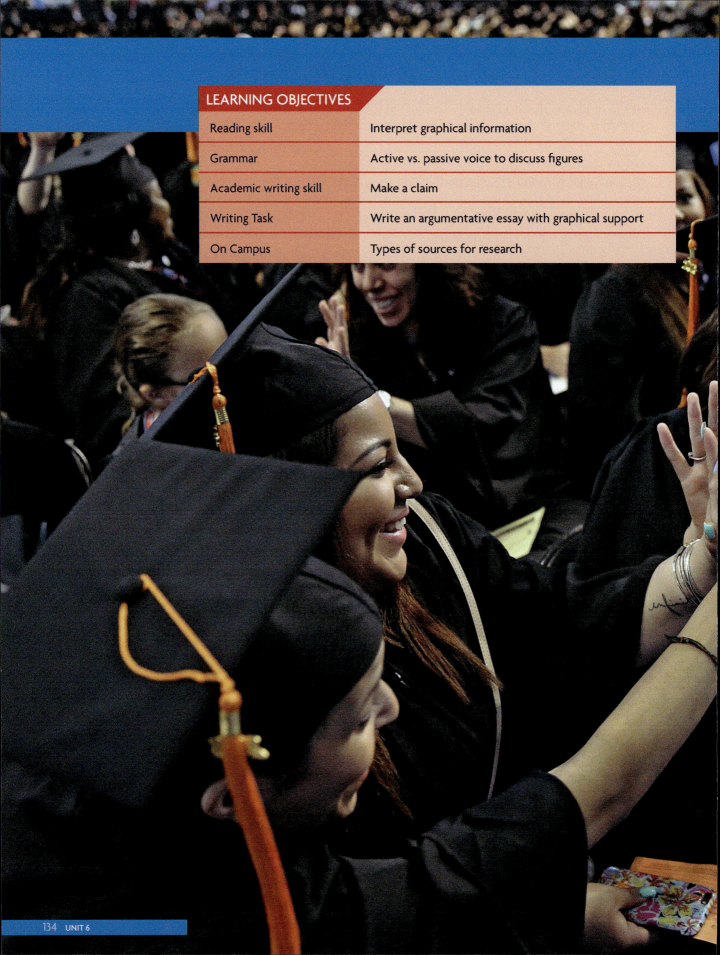

LEARNING OBJECTIVES

Reading skill	Interpret graphical information
Grammar	Active vs. passive voice to discuss figures
Academic writing skill	Make a claim
Writing Task	Write an argumentative essay with graphical support
On Campus	Types of sources for research

ACTIVATE YOUR KNOWLEDGE

Work with a partner. Discuss the questions.

1 What is happening in this picture? Have you experienced something similar?
2 What do you think is the main purpose of a college education?
3 Is college the best choice for everyone? Why or why not? What other options are there?

WATCH AND LISTEN

PREPARING TO WATCH

ACTIVATING YOUR KNOWLEDGE

1 Work with a partner. Discuss the questions.

1 Are you familiar with any specialized high schools? How is their curriculum different from a traditional high school? How might a specialized high school benefit students?

2 What do most young people do after completing high school?

3 What job opportunities exist for young people after high school?

4 What industries do you think are in need of more workers?

PREDICTING CONTENT USING VISUALS

2 Look at the images from the video. Complete the chart. Discuss your chart with a partner.

	1st image	2nd image	3rd image	4th image
1 What job does this person have?				
2 What kind of training is needed for this job?				

GLOSSARY

second shift (n) a work period that usually begins in the late afternoon and ends in the late evening (such as in a factory or hospital)

welder (n) a person whose job is joining metal parts together with high heat

hydrogen (n) the lightest gas, one of the chemical elements

instrument technician (n) a worker trained to operate specialized machines or equipment

vocational education (also known as career and technical education) (n) schooling where students learn skills that involve working with their hands

---

WHILE WATCHING

3 ▶ Watch the video. Check (✔) the ideas you hear.

UNDERSTANDING
MAIN IDEAS

1 Nick had more than one job offer when he graduated from a career and technical high school. ☐
2 The need for technical workers is increasing. ☐
3 Air Products manufactures high-tech equipment. ☐
4 John McGlade has to train the skilled workers he needs. ☐
5 Government support for vocational education is decreasing. ☐
6 Not many young people are interested in vocational education. ☐

4 ▶ Watch the video again. Write a detail for each main idea.

UNDERSTANDING
DETAILS

1 Air Products has 7,500 workers, and not all are skilled.

_____

2 John McGlade's company often has positions available.

_____

3 Career and technical education has been cut, and more cuts may be on the way.

_____

4 Vocational schools train students to work in technical careers.

_____

5 Work with a partner. Discuss the questions.

MAKING INFERENCES

1 Do you think Nick likes his job? Why or why not?
2 Why do you think John McGlade is worried?
3 Why do you think more skilled workers will be needed in the future?
4 What do you think are some other jobs that students can train for at a career and technical high school?

DISCUSSION

6 Discuss the questions with your partner.

1 Do you think entering into a career and technical high school is a good idea? Why or why not?
2 Would you have been interested in attending a career and technical high school? Why or why not?
3 What are the advantages and disadvantages of young people entering the workforce shortly after high school?

READING

READING 1

PREPARING TO READ

Interpreting graphical information

Academic texts often include charts, graphs, or other graphical elements to support and extend the content of the text.

As a first step to understanding information presented in graphical form, read the title, headings, and the labels on the axes on any graphs. This will provide some context for the information presented there. If the axes of a graph are not labeled, try to figure out what the labels would be.

PREDICTING CONTENT USING VISUALS

PRISM Digital Workbook

1 You are going to read an article about the demand for workers with appropriate skills for current and future jobs. Work with a partner. Look at this graph and discuss the questions.

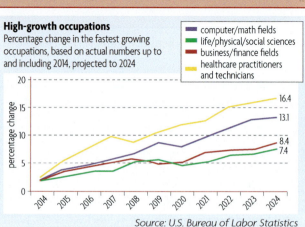

High-growth occupations
Percentage change in the fastest growing occupations, based on actual numbers up to and including 2014, projected to 2024

- computer/math fields
- life/physical/social sciences
- business/finance fields
- healthcare practitioners and technicians

Source: U.S. Bureau of Labor Statistics

1 What kinds of jobs does each category include? Name some.
2 What sorts of skills and education are required for the jobs in these fields?
3 Why do you think these occupational areas are predicted to be the fastest growing in the near future?
4 What implications might this prediction have for curriculum development in middle and high schools?

2 Now look at the graphs in Reading 1 on pages 140–141 and complete this table.

	figure 1	figure 2
What does the horizontal axis (the x axis) measure?		
What does the vertical axis (the y axis) measure?		
What information does the whole graph express?	Since 2006,	Since 2011,

3 Based on the information in the graphs in Reading 1, answer the questions.

1 Look at Figure 1. Why do you think companies are having trouble finding employees?

_____

2 What problem does Figure 2 illustrate?

_____

3 How does the information in Figure 2 explain the problems that the employers in Figure 1 are experiencing?

_____

_____

_____

4 Read the definitions. Complete the sentences with the correct form of the words in bold.

UNDERSTANDING
KEY VOCABULARY

> **alternative** (adj) different from what is usual
> **assertive** (adj) forceful; bold and confident
> **boast** (v) to talk proudly about; to have or own something to be proud of
> **expertise** (n) a high level of knowledge or skill
> **persistent** (adj) strong and determined; lasting for a long time and difficult to resolve
> **prospective** (adj) possible, especially in the future
> **qualified** (adj) having the necessary knowledge or skill
> **survey** (n) a set of questions asked of a large number of people in order to find patterns

1 Professors at this technical institute are known for their _____ in robotics and high-tech electronics.

2 It was difficult to fill the position in IT because most of the applicants really weren't _____ for the job.

3 We are conducting a _____ to find out how happy customers are with their purchases.

4 Our new campus _____ a brand new computer and technology center as well as a career placement service.

5 You have to be more _____ if you want people to take your ideas seriously.

6 Our shipping costs are way too high, so we are looking for _____ ways to deliver goods to our customers.

7 The staff in the admissions office regularly meet with _____ students to answer their questions and give campus tours.

8 For the last five years, there has been a _____ shortage of job applicants with skills in a wide range of technical areas.

THE SKILLS GAP

1   All over the country, business leaders and government officials complain about the "skills gap." Businesses have plenty of job openings, but they cannot find enough **qualified** applicants to fill the positions because workers' skills do not match those needed by employers. Figure 1 shows the results of an annual **survey** of about 42,000 companies worldwide.

2   For the most part, the employees that employers are seeking fall into two categories. The first category includes professionals in STEM fields (science / technology / engineering / mathematics) that require advanced training and **expertise**, especially in information technology (IT). The second category is much larger, comprising workers in the "skilled trades." Workers in the skilled trades have expertise in, for example, manufacturing, computers, electronics, and construction. There are simply not enough workers with training in these areas to meet the growing demand. These jobs require more than a high school education (for example, a short training program to develop the required skill), but often they do not require a college education. In the United States, almost half of the labor force works in these kinds of jobs.

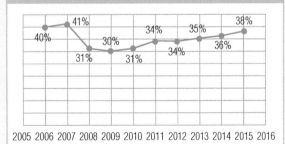

Figure 1. Percentage of companies with difficulty filling positions

41% 40% 31% 30% 31% 34% 34% 35% 36% 38%

2005 2006 2007 2008 2009 2010 2011 2012 2013 2014 2015 2016

Source: Manpower (2014)

Causes of the skills gap

3   Why have we been unable to bridge this gap and prepare workers for the jobs of the future, or even the jobs of today? The answer lies in both the job market and our educational system. The job market is changing more quickly than ever before. Many of the jobs that companies need to fill today did not exist when current job applicants were in school, making it difficult for educational programs to keep up with the demands of the market. Nevertheless, many business leaders argue that schools are not doing enough to provide the technical training that many jobs demand. For example, only a quarter of all schools in the United States teach computer science. Most schools and universities continue to offer the same type of education that they have provided in the past. As a result, many students graduate with degrees that do not prepare them for the jobs that are available. Given this mismatch between the education system and the job market, many labor experts say we cannot and perhaps should not depend on traditional schooling to close the skills gap and should instead find **alternative** solutions.

Closing the skills gap

4   Both industry and academic experts argue that businesses themselves need to take a more **assertive** role in the preparation of the labor force they require. Businesses have the best information about what skills their employees will need, so it makes sense for them to participate in training **prospective** employees. First, they need to communicate better with schools and universities about the skills they require. Second, they should establish relationships with future employees earlier, perhaps through partnership programs that begin training future employees while they are still students. Finally, businesses may need to develop and provide their own in-house training programs.

5　Technical skills, particularly IT skills, are in high demand, but developing these skills is not necessarily best accomplished by means of a traditional college education. There are a whole range of schools, courses, and training programs that have opened in response to the demand for IT professionals, some in brick-and-mortar classrooms and others online— trade schools[1] for the digital age. The top IT schools are expensive, but some **boast** a 99% placement rate for their graduates, many of whom find positions that pay $100,000 a year or more. Figure 2 displays the predicted job growth in computing jobs.

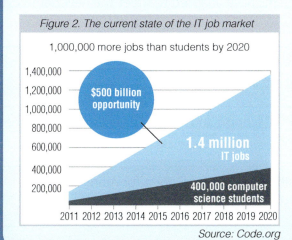

Figure 2. The current state of the IT job market

1,000,000 more jobs than students by 2020

$500 billion opportunity

1.4 million IT jobs

400,000 computer science students

2011 2012 2013 2014 2015 2016 2017 2018 2019 2020

Source: Code.org

6　The skills gap is both **persistent** and expensive. One business expert estimates that a company loses $14,000 when a position remains open for three months. The skills gap is the result of many factors, and there is no single solution to the problems it poses. It is likely that a combination of approaches will be needed before the supply of qualified workers will be able to meet demand for them.

[1]**trade school** (n) a school where students learn the skills for a job such as electrician, mechanic, or chef

WHILE READING

5 Read the article. Then match the main ideas to each paragraph.

READING FOR MAIN IDEAS

Main ideas	Paragraph
a Schools that provide training in IT can help fill the skills gap.	_____
b Employees in the skilled trades and with STEM training are in the greatest demand.	_____
c There is no single solution to the skills gap.	_____
d Current job applicants do not have the skills that employees are looking for.	_____
e Businesses need to participate more in preparing future employees.	_____
f Colleges do not always offer an education with a clear career path.	_____

6 Read the article again. Which of the statements in Exercise 5 expresses the main idea of the whole text? _____

7 Read the article again. Write *T* (true), *F* (false), or *DNS* (does not say) for each statement below. Correct the false statements.

_____ **1** Globalization has led to labor shortages in some developing countries.

_____

_____ **2** The most critical labor shortages are in IT fields.

_____

_____ **3** The positions that companies are trying to fill all require a college education.

_____

_____ **4** About 50% of workers in the United States are in the skilled trades.

_____

_____ **5** Education programs have adapted to meet the new demand for technical skills.

_____

_____ **6** Businesses have the most accurate knowledge of the kinds of employees that are in demand.

_____

_____ **7** More than 1,000 IT schools and training programs have opened to meet demand.

_____

_____ **8** An unfilled position that remains open for more than three months can cost a company more than $10,000.

_____

READING BETWEEN THE LINES

8 Work with a partner. Answer the questions.

1 What is the purpose of this article?
  a to persuade colleges to change their programs
  b to help job candidates
  c to offer general information
  d to warn employers

2 Where might you find an article like this?
  a in a print or online magazine
  b in a textbook
  c on Wikipedia
  d in an academic journal

DISCUSSION

9 Work with a partner. Discuss the questions.

1 What do you think is the $500 billion opportunity in Figure 2?
2 Do you think the trends shown in the graphs will continue in the future? Why or why not?
3 Who do you think should take action to improve this situation?

READING 2

PREPARING TO READ

PREDICTING CONTENT USING VISUALS

1 Work with a partner. You are going to read an article about the value of a college education. Study the graphs in Reading 2 on page 145. Then discuss the questions. After you read the article, come back and check your ideas.

1 Based on Figure 1, what generalization can you make about college education?

2 Look at Figure 2. What does *median income* mean? Are college-educated workers more likely to earn above or below the median income?

3 What do you think the topic of this article will be? What argument do you think it will make?

UNDERSTANDING KEY VOCABULARY

2 Read the sentences and write the words in bold next to the definitions.

1 My father suffers from **chronic** pain. He never complains, but I know his back hurts all the time.

2 Steve Jobs was one of the **founders** of Apple, Inc.

3 Business leaders **dispute** the government's claim that the number of jobs has grown.

4 The current protests are an **illustration** of the continuing importance of free speech.

5 There is some **ambiguity** in the law, so it is difficult to know whether the company actually did anything wrong.

6 This new technology has the **potential** to change how students learn about science.

7 The impact of the war on the economy eventually **diminished**, but it took a long time.

8 The consequences of this disaster **extend** beyond the city to the whole country.

a _____ (v) to disagree with

b _____ (n) the state of being unclear or having more than one possible meaning

c _____ (n) people who establish an organization

d _____ (v) to decrease in size or importance

e _____ (adj) lasting for a long time, especially something bad

f _____ (v) to go further

g _____ (n) the possibility to develop and succeed

h _____ (n) an example that explains something

PRISM Digital Workbook

WHILE READING

3 Read the article. Write *T* (true), *F* (false), or *DNS* (does not say) for each statement below. Correct the false statements.

_____ 1 A college education is worth the investment.

_____

_____ 2 College graduates in the U.S. make twice as much as those with just a high school degree.

_____

_____ 3 College graduates generally have healthier lifestyles than those without a college degree.

_____

_____ 4 College graduates are more likely to vote than those without a college degree.

_____

_____ 5 Liberal arts graduates have higher incomes than graduates with an engineering degree.

_____

_____ 6 Liberal arts graduates offer some advantages over graduates with technical degrees.

_____

4 Read the article again. Which of the statements in Exercise 3 expresses the main idea of the whole text? _____

5 Refer to the graphs in Reading 2 to answer the questions.

Figure 1
1 Which country had the highest percentage of college graduates in 2012? _____
2 Which country had the largest increase in the percentage of college graduates between 2000 and 2012? _____
3 What percentage of the Mexican population (25–64) had a college degree in 2012? _____

Figure 2
1 Which country had the highest percentage of college graduates with incomes more than twice the median? _____
2 Which country had the highest number of college graduates with incomes at the country median or below? _____
3 What percentage of the college graduates in Brazil earned more than twice the median income? _____

What Is the Value of a College Education?

1 A college education is a significant investment, so it makes sense to consider carefully whether it is worth the time and money. In good economic times and bad, and in spite of its rising cost, the answer is "yes." According to the Organisation for Economic Cooperation and Development (OECD), around the world the number of people getting a college education is rising steadily (see Figure 1).

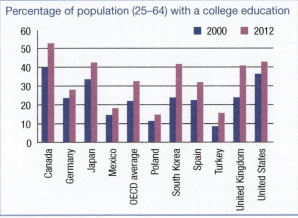

Figure 1   *Source: OECD Indicators*

The impact of a college education

2 A college education has a broad and positive impact. People with a college degree are by far the most likely to enter and remain in the labor force. In OECD countries, average participation in the labor force for those who never completed high school is about 55%. For those with a high school degree, the figure is about 70%, and for college graduates, it is about 83%. College graduates also earn more than those with only a high school degree. In the United States, a new high school graduate earned on average $28,000 per year in 2013, whereas those with a college degree made about $45,000. Over a lifetime, that difference adds up to about a million dollars. Figure 2 provides a dramatic **illustration** of the impact of a college degree on income in selected OECD countries.

3 The consequences of getting—or not getting—a college education **extend** beyond income. There is a strong association between education and health. **Chronic** diseases, such as heart disease and diabetes, pose the greatest risks to public health in developed countries today. These diseases are caused, at least partly, by lifestyle choices, such as poor diet or smoking. In general, people with higher levels of education make healthier lifestyle choices and have greater access to high-quality healthcare.

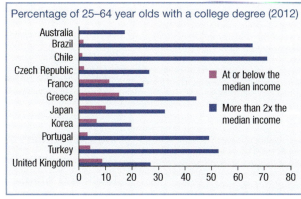

Figure 2   *Source: OECD Indicators*

Income variance between degrees

4 It is evident that a college degree provides an economic advantage, but not all degrees have the same earning power. Most analyses suggest that degrees in STEM fields (science, technology, engineering, and math) have the greatest **potential** impact on future income. In the United States, a college graduate with, for example, a chemical engineering degree can expect to earn about $70,000 annually, whereas a graduate with a literature or art degree may be lucky to get $36,000 for an entry-level position. Marc Andreessen, the **founder** of the Internet company Netscape, once declared that someone who studies a non-technical field like literature will probably end up "working in a shoe store."

5 Yet, technical knowledge alone may not be sufficient for success. Steve Jobs, one of the founders of Apple, famously claimed, "It's technology married with liberal arts … that yields the results that make our hearts sing." Other major employers in the technology field agree. Industry leaders say employees from the liberal arts are good at managing **ambiguity**, unlike engineers, who tend to see situations in black and white. Liberal arts graduates can see a problem from multiple perspectives.

6 It is interesting to note that the income gap between liberal arts and STEM graduates gradually **diminishes** as they continue in their careers. In fact, liberal arts degrees are quite common among the world's most highly paid workers. About one-third of the directors of Fortune 500 companies[1] have a liberal arts background. Students, parents, politicians, and industry leaders may argue over which are the most valuable degrees, but the value of a college degree in general cannot be **disputed**.

[1]**Fortune 500 companies** (n) the businesses ranked by *Fortune* magazine as the 500 most profitable companies in the U.S. for a particular year

READING BETWEEN THE LINES

MAKING INFERENCES

6 Work with a partner. Discuss the questions.

1 What relationship, if any, exists among education, income, and health?
2 What do you think Steve Jobs meant by "the results that make our hearts sing"?
3 Based on this excerpt from Reading 2, what are some jobs that liberal arts graduates would be good at? Why?

> Industry leaders say employees from the liberal arts are good at managing ambiguity, unlike engineers, who tend to see situations in black and white.

DISCUSSION

SYNTHESIZING

7 Work with a partner or in small groups. Use ideas from Reading 1 and Reading 2 to discuss the questions.

1 Do you think that future income should be the primary factor in deciding on a course of study? Why or why not?
2 Why do you think the impact of a college education on income is greater in some countries than in others?
3 Should everyone have to study technology? Why or why not?
4 Some politicians have suggested that only students who are preparing for careers that help to close the skills gap should get financial aid from the government. Do you agree? Why or why not?

⊙ LANGUAGE DEVELOPMENT

COMPLEX NOUN PHRASES

LANGUAGE

English, especially academic English, often uses nouns to modify other nouns. These noun + noun phrases can take many forms:

Compound nouns: healthcare, lifestyle
Separate words: skills gap, stress level
Gerund + noun: leading indicator, operating costs

There are also noun + noun + noun phrases, but these are less common:

student identification number
application cover letter

1 Choose one noun from each box to complete the sentences.

first noun		second noun	
earning	placement	balance	market
entry	training	force	power
job	work–life	level	program
labor		rate	

1 The city community college offers a _____ _____ for people who hope to become airplane mechanics.

2 Statistics clearly demonstrate that a college degree increases lifetime _____ _____ .

3 Our program has an excellent _____ _____ . More than 90% of our graduates find a job within a month.

4 The _____ _____ has been very weak this year, as can be seen from the steady increase in unemployment.

5 The _____ _____ is defined as all the people in the population who are able to work.

6 Recent college graduates usually join a business at the _____ _____ , but some graduates with a STEM background are able to find more senior positions.

7 Salary is an important consideration in choosing a career, but a career that offers a good _____ _____ is just as important.

2 Unscramble the words to create complex noun phrases. Then use them correctly in the sentences below.

a information / professional / technology   _____

b training / graduate / program   _____

c participation / rate / force / labor   _____

d enrollment / trends / college   _____

e household / income / median   _____

1 The _____ in the United States is just over $50,000 per year.

2 A local car parts factory announced that it will hire its first _____ this summer.

3 If you want a secure future, you may want to consider a career as a(n) _____ .

4 The _____ in the United States has fluctuated between 60% and 70% in the past ten years.

5 The U.S. Department of Education keeps track of _____ and reports their data every year.

WRITING

CRITICAL THINKING

At the end of this unit, you are going to write an argumentative essay about factors that are important in choosing a career. Your essay should include some form of graphical support. Look at this unit's Writing Task below.

> Considering what you know about the job market, what is a good choice for a career path with a secure future?

Analyzing information in graphs and other figures

Information in academic texts is often presented visually in graphs or other types of figures. It is important to be able to connect this information with the information in the text.

UNDERSTAND

1 Work with a partner. Read the information about the annual 100 Best Jobs report and study the figure. Take turns explaining each of the components in your own words.

> Every year, the news magazine *U.S. News and World Report* publishes a report on the year's 100 best jobs. Figure 5 shows how the report's authors measured job quality.

Figure 5. **Components of *Best Job* measure**

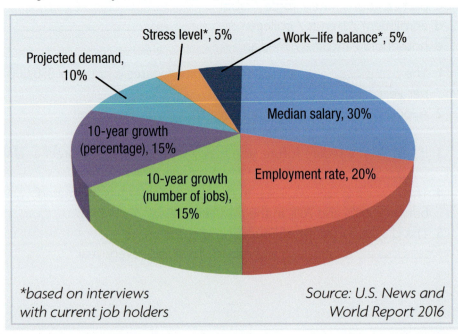

Stress level*, 5%

Work–life balance*, 5%

Projected demand, 10%

10-year growth (percentage), 15%

Median salary, 30%

10-year growth (number of jobs), 15%

Employment rate, 20%

*based on interviews with current job holders

Source: U.S. News and World Report 2016

2 With your partner, complete the tasks.

1 Table 1, below, is a selection from the 100 Best Jobs list along with the median salaries for each job. Based on what you have learned in this unit, explain the wide range of median salaries for the jobs in the table.

2 The highest ranked job is also the highest paid, but this relationship is not consistent throughout the list. Choose two examples and explain what other components in the measure could be responsible for the ranking.

Table 1. **The 100 best jobs in the U.S., with median salary**

Rank	job title	median salary
2	Dentist	$150,000
13	Software Developer	$96,000
22	Nurse	$67,000
24	Accountant	$66,000
36	Pharmacist	$121,000
38	Mechanical Engineer	$83,000
49	Medical Secretary	$32,000
66	Laboratory Technician	$38,000
71	Lawyer	$71,000
73	Social Worker	$52,000
81	High School Teacher	$56,000
84	Insurance Salesperson	$48,000
91	Manicurist	$20,000
93	Anthropologist	$59,000

Source: U.S. News and World Report 2016

3 Think of another job, perhaps your own job or one that you would like.

1 Give the approximate ranking that you think this job would get. Give reasons for your ranking.

2 What do you think is the salary potential for this job? Why?

ACTIVE VS. PASSIVE VOICE TO DISCUSS FIGURES

Within an academic text, supporting images and graphical elements (graphs, charts, diagrams) are usually all referred to as *figures*.

When writers discuss figures, they use specific words and phrases, sometimes in the passive voice.

To introduce a trend by discussing a figure, the active voice is usually preferred.
Every year, the news magazine *U.S. News and World Report* publishes a report about the year's 100 best jobs. Figure 5 **shows** how the report's authors measured job quality.

If you have already introduced a trend, the passive may be a better choice to avoid repetition.

Judgment of job quality has several components. These **are presented** in Figure 5.

These verbs are frequently used when discussing figures:

demonstrate	*depict*	*display*
illustrate	*indicate*	*portray*
present	*reveal*	*show*

PRISM Digital Workbook

1 Work with a partner. Match the figures to their descriptions. Write *A*, *B*, *C*, or *D*.

Figure A. Reasons for the skills gap

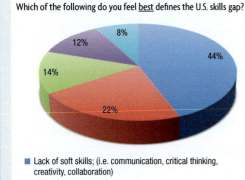

Which of the following do you feel <u>best</u> defines the U.S. skills gap?

- 44%
- 22%
- 14%
- 12%
- 8%

- ■ Lack of soft skills; (i.e. communication, critical thinking, creativity, collaboration)
- ■ Lack of technical skills
- ■ Lack of strong leadership skills
- ■ Lack of computer based technology skills
- ■ N/A – I do not think there is a skills gap in the U.S. workforce

Adecco

Source: Adecco 2013

Figure B. U.S. labor force participation

Source: Washington Post/Bureau of Labor Statistics 2013

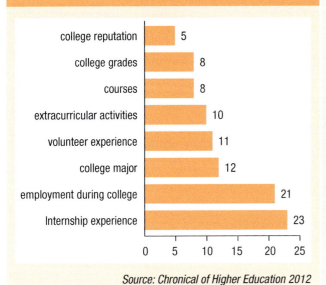

Figure C. How employers weigh factors when they evaluate college graduates on a scale of 1–25

college reputation 5
college grades 8
courses 8
extracurricular activities 10
volunteer experience 11
college major 12
employment during college 21
Internship experience 23

Source: Chronical of Higher Education 2012

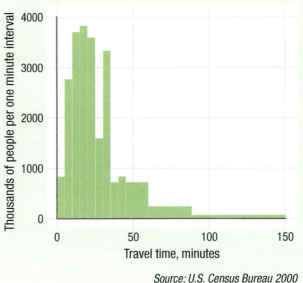

Figure D. Usual time of daily commute to work

Source: U.S. Census Bureau 2000

1 A *line graph* usually shows change over time. _____
2 A *pie chart* shows the proportion that each category in the chart represents, usually as percentages of a whole. _____
3 A *histogram* displays frequency data, usually in columns, with the Y axis as the counter. _____
4 A *bar graph* compares the amounts or frequency of categories that are not part of a whole. _____

2 Which sentence best expresses the content of each figure in Exercise 1? Write A, B, C, or D. Notice the words in bold used.

1 Employer preference for experience over academic preparation **is clearly indicated** by Figure _____ .
2 Figure _____ **depicts** the steep rise in labor force participation during the final quarter of the 20th century.
3 The length of time employees spend going to and from work in a normal day **is shown** in Figure _____ .
4 Figure _____ **presents** the results of a survey of 500 major employers regarding their views on the skills gap.

3 For each of the figures in Reading 1 and Reading 2, write one sentence that summarizes the information and one sentence that introduces the material in the graph. You may write them in either order. Pay attention to passive and active voice. Compare your sentences with a partner.

Making a claim

In an argumentative essay, a writer makes a claim and then provides support for that claim. The claim is delivered in the thesis statement. So the claim is the writer's argument, and the thesis statement is the way that argument is expressed in words.

An effective thesis statement does several things:
- It gives readers an idea of what the paper will be about, but it does *not* list every supporting idea that will be offered.
- It narrows down a broader topic so that the writer can fully explore it in an essay.
- It helps readers understand and interpret information about the topic.
- It presents a claim that readers could argue with. For this reason, facts do not make effective claims.

The thesis statement will generally appear in the first paragraph of an essay. Usually it is expressed in a single sentence, but a complex claim may require two sentences.

To check if you have written an effective thesis statement, ask yourself these questions:
- Does my thesis statement make a claim that my readers can argue about?
- Does it give readers an idea of what my paper will be about without listing every point?
- Is the claim specific enough to be effectively supported in a short essay?

PRISM Digital Workbook

1 Choose the best thesis statement for an essay about the skills gap in the labor market.

   a The skills gap is an economic problem that has developed over several decades.
   b Addressing the skills gap will require significant changes in the education system and the participation of the business community.
   c The skills gap is a consequence of the changing economy.
   d We understand the cause of the skills gap; now it is time to find a way to end it.
   e The skills gap has developed because the job market changed, schools are not providing training in technical areas, and businesses have not communicated their needs to educational leaders.

2 Work with a partner. Review the thesis statements in Exercise 1. For each one, answer the questions.

   1 Does the statement make a claim? If so, what is it?
   2 Is the claim something readers could argue about?
   3 Is the claim specific enough to be developed in a short essay?
   4 Are there other reasons the sentence is not an effective thesis statement?

WRITING TASK

PRISM Digital Workbook

Considering what you know about the job market, what is a good choice for a career path with a secure future?

PLAN

1 Gather information for your essay by rereading the two articles in this unit and making notes in the chart below.

	Reading 1	Reading 2
main point		
introduction		
section 1		
section 2		

2 Work with a partner. Discuss possible claims for your essays. Make notes about your discussion.

1 What is the best career path? _____

2 What considerations are you basing your claim on? Considerations may include:

- form of education needed (college, high school, vocational training)
- if college is needed, type of major
- salary potential
- market demand—which positions are in demand now and will continue to be in demand in the future
- job satisfaction factors

3 Write a thesis statement for your essay.

1 Review your notes from the previous exercise and the questions from Academic Writing Skills, Exercise 2. What claim do you want to make?

_____

_____

2 How will you express that claim in a thesis statement?

_____

_____

_____

4 Organize the body paragraphs of your essay.

1 Highlight the notes in your chart (page 153) that support your claim.

2 Organize the notes into groups around themes or topics by numbering, circling, or highlighting them in different colors. Topics might include:
   - current and future trends in the labor market
   - salary potential
   - educational requirements
   - work–life balance

   Choose two or three topics to write about in your essay.

3 Decide on the order of your topics. Write a topic sentence for each of your body paragraphs.

First body paragraph: _____

_____

_____

Second body paragraph: _____

_____

_____

Third body paragraph: _____

_____

_____

4 Choose a figure from the unit, or find or create one of your own, to help explain a supporting point in one of your body paragraphs. Write a sentence that explains what your chosen figure shows. (see Grammar for Writing, Exercise 3)

_____

_____

_____

5 Think about your conclusion. What thoughts do you want to leave your readers with?

6 Refer to the Task Checklist on page 155 as you prepare your essay.

WRITE A FIRST DRAFT

7 Write your argumentative essay based on your essay plan. Write 500–600 words.

REVISE

8 Use the Task Checklist to review your essay for content and structure.

TASK CHECKLIST	✔
Have you introduced and explained your topic?	
Does your thesis statement make a claim that people could argue about?	
Have you paraphrased the information in the articles in your own words?	
Do your body paragraphs have topic sentences?	
Do your body paragraphs support your claim?	
Have you included a figure to support at least one of the points in your essay?	
Does your concluding paragraph leave your readers with something to think about?	

9 Make any necessary changes to your essay.

EDIT

10 Use the Language Checklist to edit your essay for language errors.

LANGUAGE CHECKLIST	✔
Have you used complex noun phrases correctly in your essay?	
Did you use appropriate verbs to introduce information from graphics?	
Did you use active and passive voice correctly to introduce or refer to information shown in graphics?	
Did you give your graphics a figure number and title? Did you cite the source below it?	

11 Make any necessary changes to your essay.

TYPES OF SOURCES FOR RESEARCH

PREPARING TO READ

1 Work with a partner. Discuss the questions.

  1 What kind of sources do you usually use when you are writing a paper?
  2 Have you ever written a paper based on your own research or a survey that you did? What other sources did you use?
  3 How would documents like old diaries, letters, or photographs be useful in research?

WHILE READING

2 Read the chart on the next page from a reference library website describing different types of sources and how two researchers use them. Then categorize the sources below.

a letters from soldiers	**d** an analysis of a study on hand washing
b an encyclopedia article on good bacteria	**e** new data on Zika virus vaccines
c a list of soldiers killed in battle	**f** a scholarly book about women in the Civil War

	Daniel	Hiroko
primary		
secondary		
tertiary		

3 Work with a partner. Compare the sources used by Daniel and Hiroko in their respective fields. How are they similar? How are they different?

PRACTICE

4 With your partner, classify the sources as *P* (primary), *S* (secondary), or *T* (tertiary).

  1 a 1973 newspaper article about job trends _____
  2 commentary on a study on job loyalty _____
  3 a book about worker retention _____
  4 *Occupational Outlook Handbook*, U.S. Bureau of Labor _____
  5 an analysis of a government employment report _____
  6 *Career and Occupations Guide* _____
  7 a dissertation on outsourcing jobs _____
  8 the results from new research on job satisfaction _____

	Description	**Examples**
Primary	Original texts or media from the people directly involved and from the time period involved.	letters, diaries, speeches, photographs, artwork, surveys, interviews, original research, government data
Secondary	Commentary, interpretation, or analysis of primary sources; usually published.	biographies, journal articles, and books based on primary sources; reviews and commentaries
Tertiary	Texts of factual information but no analysis: summaries, condensed versions of secondary or primary sources.	dictionaries, encyclopedias, handbooks, tables, compilations

I'm a graduate student in humanities[1], specifically history, and my thesis is on the American Civil War. For primary sources, I read a lot of diaries from that period. I also study photographs by Matthew Brady, a famous photographer from that era. For secondary sources, I mostly read biographies written by other scholars. When I need basic factual information, like lists of officers at a battle, I look for a tertiary source like *The Civil War Dictionary*. I also use tertiary sources for background information when I start a project. —————————— **Daniel**

I'm a researcher in microbiology. The most useful sources for my work are primary sources: reports with new scientific ideas or data written by the scientists themselves. Articles that analyze or summarize the results of those experiments are secondary sources. Both primary and secondary sources are peer reviewed[2]. I use tertiary sources for common information, like chemical reactions or formulas. These are usually in science dictionaries and encyclopedias. —————————— **Hiroko**

[1]**humanities** (n) courses of study that involve human experience, such as history, languages, literature, religion, art, and music
[2]**peer reviewed** (adj) checked by experts in the same field

REAL-WORLD APPLICATION

5 Choose one of these topics for a hypothetical research paper:

Women and careers in science How technology affects career choices
Careers in the U.S. since 1970 Attitudes of millennials about careers

Go to the campus library and ask a reference librarian for guidance with your search for sources. Share your results with the class.

  1 One primary source: _____
  2 One secondary source: _____
  3 One tertiary source: _____

LEARNING OBJECTIVES

Reading skill	Recognize discourse organization
Grammar	Cause and effect: logical connectors
Academic writing skill	Write about causes and effects
Writing Task	Write a cause-and-effect essay
On Campus	Applying to a degree program

ACTIVATE YOUR KNOWLEDGE

Work with a partner. Discuss the questions.

1 What do you think is happening in this photo?

2 Which diseases do you think are the greatest threats to global health today?

3 Do you think the world's population is healthier now than a hundred years ago? Why or why not?

4 The world's population is more interconnected than ever before. What effect do you think this has on global health?

WATCH AND LISTEN

   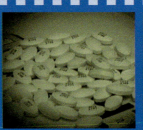 

PREPARING TO WATCH

ACTIVATING YOUR KNOWLEDGE

1 Work with a partner. Discuss the questions.

1 Have you ever gotten really sick from something you ate? What type of food was it? How long were you sick?
2 What types of food are more likely to cause illness?
3 What steps do you take to prevent food poisoning and other food-related illnesses?

PREDICTING CONTENT USING VISUALS

2 Look at the pictures from the video. Discuss the questions with your partner.

1 What do you think is being studied or researched?
2 Are you familiar with the CDC (Centers for Disease Control and Prevention)? What do you think their role is?
3 Who develops new treatments or medicines? How long do you think it takes to develop new medicines?

GLOSSARY

agonizing (adj) causing extreme physical or mental pain

E. coli (n) a type of bacteria that lives in the intestines of humans and other animals, and causes severe illness

contaminate (v) to make something less pure or make it toxic

mutation (n) a change that happens in an organism's genes that can be passed to new organisms by reproduction, or the process of this change

superbug (n) a type of bacteria that causes an illness that cannot be cured by antibiotics

lethal strain (n phr) a deadly virus that is only slightly different from other viruses of the same type

skyrocket (v) to rise extremely quickly

WHILE WATCHING

3 ▶ Watch the video. Write *T* (true) or *F* (false) next to the statements. Correct the false statements.

_____ 1 Tom Dukes had emergency surgery due to an E. coli virus he became infected with.

_____

_____ 2 Superbugs develop genes that are resistant to current antibiotics.

_____

_____ 3 Antibiotics are often unnecessarily prescribed.

_____

_____ 4 Pharmaceutical companies can develop new drugs in a short amount of time.

_____

4 ▶ Watch the video again. Complete each sentence.

1 Before contracting E. coli from contaminated meat, Tom Dukes ...

_____

2 According to Dr. Spellberg, drug-resistant superbugs begin as ...

_____

3 A recent study documented an overuse of antibiotics, noting that ...

_____

4 Drug companies are investing more money into the drugs ...

_____

5 Work with a partner. Discuss the questions.

1 What effects has E. coli had on Tom's life?
2 Why do you think there has been an increase in cases of people contracting E. coli from contaminated foods?
3 What do you think are the reasons antibiotics are overprescribed?

DISCUSSION

6 Discuss the questions with your partner.

1 Do you think the emergence of a drug-resistant bacteria is a public health crisis? Why or why not?
2 Why do you think it takes so long and costs so much money to develop a new antibiotic?
3 Do you think it is important to invest more money into the research and development of new antibiotics? Why or why not? Who should pay for more research and development?

READING

READING 1

PREPARING TO READ

1 You are going to read an article about superbugs. Work with a partner. Discuss the questions.

1 When you are feeling sick and go to a doctor's office or clinic, do you usually get antibiotics? Why or why not?
2 Do you always finish all the medication the doctor prescribes even if you are feeling better? Why or why not?
3 Why do you think antibiotics are commonly given to livestock, that is, animals that produce food for humans?

2 Read the sentences and choose the best definition for the words in bold.

1 The Internet has **revolutionized** almost everything we do, from shopping to studying.
   a made easier
   b completely changed
   c made more accessible
2 The news report presented a **grim** picture of the life and experiences of the war refugees.
   a very bad; worrisome
   b dangerous
   c conflicting; unclear
3 Mosquitoes **thrive** in warm, wet conditions, so they are more common in summer.
   a live and develop successfully
   b compete with each other more easily
   c struggle to survive
4 Everyone gets sick now and then, but people who are healthy usually **bounce back** quickly.
   a have problems
   b consult a professional
   c return to normal
5 Business **cycles** involve periods of economic expansion, followed by downturns, and then periods of expansion again.
   a office environments
   b publications
   c repeating series of events

6 Scientists have discovered that some common plants have **therapeutic** properties. Chemicals from the plants are beneficial to patients with a variety of conditions.

    a economic   **b** substantial   **c** healing

7 City workers are spraying chemicals in wet areas to **counter** the recent increase in the mosquito population. City officials worry that these insects may spread diseases.

    a defend against   **b** investigate   **c** keep track of

8 He had a very **mild** case of the flu, so he was able to go back to work after only a few days.

    a not contagious   **b** not extreme   **c** not pleasant

WHILE READING

3 Read the article on page 164. Which of these statements best expresses the main idea of the article?

READING FOR
MAIN IDEAS

    a Bacteria will always find a way to get around antibiotics.

    b Antibiotics in the food chain have led to the spread of drug-resistant bacteria.

    c The misuse of antibiotics is a primary factor in the rise of drug-resistant bacteria.

    d Since our strongest antibiotics are powerless against the latest strain of bacteria, we should expect more outbreaks of dangerous diseases.

SKILLS

Recognizing discourse organization

Essays are usually organized to meet general goals. An essay may

- describe a process
- compare and/or contrast two or more things
- describe the causes or consequences of things
- explain how something works
- describe a system of classification
- relate a series of events

Recognizing these discourse patterns can help you predict and comprehend the content of a text.

---

4 Which discourse pattern best describes Reading 1?

PRISM Digital Workbook

_____

SUPERBUGS

1 They are so small that you need a microscope to see them, but so powerful that they kill an average of 37,000 people in the United States every year. They are superbugs—drug-resistant bacteria that have emerged since antibiotics **revolutionized** medicine in the early 20th century. Indeed, the rise of these superbugs and the use of antibiotics are closely intertwined.

2 All organisms change over time; this is a basic principle of evolution. Smaller organisms, such as bacteria, are able to evolve more quickly, adapting as circumstances require. In the face of antibiotics, bacteria have adapted with deadly efficiency. When a patient takes antibiotics to fight off a bacterial infection, the goal is to kill the bacteria causing the infection. Often, however, although most of the bacteria are killed, a few of the strongest bacteria survive. Thus, only these drug-resistant bacteria are able to reproduce. This sets up a **cycle** in which increasingly powerful antibiotics are needed to **counter** bacterial infections, eventually resulting in the development of superbugs—bacteria able to resist even the most powerful drugs.

3 Scientists believe that a large part of this cycle is preventable. Few would dispute that patients who are genuinely ill should take antibiotics, but one recent study suggested that almost 50% of all antibiotic use is inappropriate or unnecessary. Some patients take antibiotics for ailments that would eventually clear up on their own, or for viral infections, against which antibiotics have no effect. In addition, some patients do not finish their course of medication, allowing bacteria to **bounce back**, but stronger. All of these factors contribute to the rise and spread of superbugs. Although many doctors find it difficult to refuse when patients request medication, in this instance, what may be safe and effective for the individual can be harmful to society as a whole.

4 Another major factor that promotes the spread of drug resistance is the use of antibiotics for livestock. The Natural Resources Defense Council reports that 80% of antibiotic use in the United States is for animals. In part, the drugs are used to prevent the spread of infection among animals, especially those that live in crowded conditions. However, farmers also use antibiotics because these drugs help animals to gain weight quickly. Unfortunately, such non-**therapeutic** use of antibiotics is problematic because it kills off the beneficial bacteria that normally lives in the animals' digestive tract, leaving drug-resistant strains of bacteria to **thrive**.

5 The widespread use of antibiotics for the past 70 years in both the animal and human populations, and the resulting increase in drug-resistant bacteria, have fueled an ongoing search for more powerful drugs. In the early days of antibiotic research, scientists were successful in finding new classes of drugs, capable of fighting the drug-resistant bacteria that continually appeared. Since then, however, drug discovery has tapered off to almost nothing (see Figure 1). Very few weapons remain against the deadliest bacteria. Late in 2015, researchers reported the emergence of a strain of bacteria able to resist even the most powerful medications, those only used as a last resort.

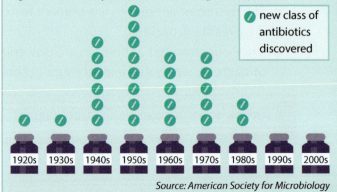

Figure 1. The history of anti-bacterial drug development

🔵 new class of antibiotics discovered

1920s 1930s 1940s 1950s 1960s 1970s 1980s 1990s 2000s

Source: American Society for Microbiology

6 What can be done to stop this cycle? Scientists maintain that as individuals, we can make a difference with simple steps, such as regular hand washing. It is also important that patients understand that antibiotics are not always the right course of treatment. They should not be taken for viral infections or even for **mild** bacterial infections. Finally, it is crucial to take antibiotics out of the food chain. Fortunately, consumers are pushing for this, so we are likely to see changes in this practice in the near future. The fast food giant McDonald's, which sells millions of pounds of chicken every year, has begun using only antibiotic-free chicken. If both individuals and corporations around the world continue to take steps like these, perhaps superbugs can be stopped. The alternative presents a **grim** picture for future generations.

5 Read the article again. Label the events in the causal chain of drug resistance.

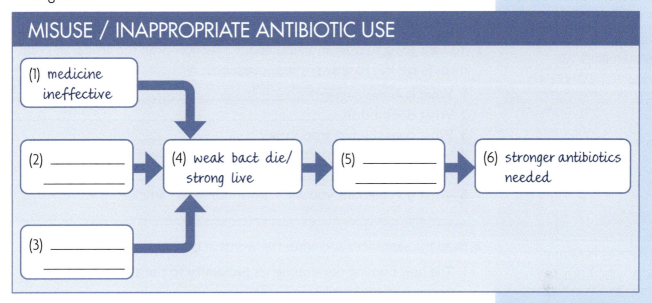

READING BETWEEN THE LINES

6 Find these phrases in Reading 1. Try to infer their meaning from context and match them to the correct definition below.

1 closely intertwined (para 1)
2 in the face of (para 2)
3 on their own (para 3)
4 taper off (para 5)
5 as a last resort (para 5)

a without help
b connected; difficult to separate
c gradually become weaker or happen less often
d when every other option has failed
e when threatened by

7 Work with a partner. Write a sentence for each phrase in Exercise 6, using the phrase in context correctly. Share your sentences with the class.

DISCUSSION

8 Work with a partner. Discuss the questions.

1 Look back at Figure 1 in the text. What does it show? What do you think will happen in the future?
2 Some farmers argue that antibiotics prevent their animals from getting sick and ensure that the meat they produce is safe for humans. Do you think this is a good reason to give these drugs to healthy animals? Why or why not?
3 Should patients be able to demand medication from a doctor if it might help but isn't absolutely necessary? Think about a parent with a sick child. Explain your answer.

READING 2

PREPARING TO READ

SCANNING TO PREDICT CONTENT

1 You are going to read an article about infection. Scan the article and the maps (page 167) to answer these questions.

1 What is *Aedes aegypti*? _____

2 What does it do? _____

3 What does the first map show? _____

4 How does the U.S. habitat of *Aedes aegypti* differ from that of *Aedes albopictus*? _____

5 What do you think you will learn about in this article?

_____

UNDERSTANDING KEY VOCABULARY

PRISM Digital Workbook

2 Read the sentences and write the words in bold next to the definitions.

1 The new housing development's **proximity** to the airport is a problem because of the noise.

2 The military uses a secret code for the **transmission** of messages from headquarters to soldiers in the field.

3 The damage from the fire was **confined** to the third and fourth floors of the building.

4 It is not possible to **eradicate** some diseases, but it is possible to control them.

5 Social media sites **facilitate** the sharing of information. News can spread around the globe in an instant.

6 Early **detection** of cancer can substantially improve the chances of recovery.

7 There has been a **surge** in complaints about dangerous chemicals in the drinking water since farm animals started mysteriously dying.

8 Many rural populations depend on **domesticated** animals for food and labor.

a _____ (n) the notice or discovery of something

b _____ (n) nearness

c _____ (n) a sudden, large increase

d _____ (v) to make something possible or easier

e _____ (n) the process of passing something from one person or place to another

f _____ (v) to exist in or apply to a limited group or area

g _____ (adj) under human control; used for animals

h _____ (v) to get rid of something completely

THE GLOBALIZATION OF INFECTION

1 Recent headlines have been filled with alarming news of the spread of pathogens[1] that cause diseases like SARS, MERS, swine flu, dengue fever, chikungunya, and the latest—the Zika virus. Are these pathogens really on the increase, or have **detection** and reporting methods simply improved? In fact, several studies suggest that the **surge** in these infectious diseases is quite real. Researchers propose a number of reasons for these developments.

2 Probably the most obvious reason is how closely connected the world has become. Human populations regularly travel long distances as immigrants, business travelers, or tourists, carrying diseases with them. For example, it is thought that the Zika virus may have traveled from French Polynesia to Brazil in the blood of infected international athletes. People are not the only world travelers; insects, primarily mosquitoes, can also hop on a boat or a plane and migrate thousands of miles. Scientists refer to the hosts that carry pathogens as *vectors*. When they bite, vectors transfer infected blood to a new victim, spreading the pathogen in both humans and animal populations. As these vectors move around the world, and if they can survive and reproduce in their new environment, the range of the disease grows.

3 The pathogens themselves are also highly adaptable. Most pathogens are found in a specific vector. For example, chikungunya is carried by a particular type of mosquito, *Aedes aegypti*, in Africa and Asia, where the disease originated. As the virus traveled across the Pacific, however, it mutated[2] to a new form, which thrives in a different vector, the Asian Tiger mosquito, *Aedes albopictus*, allowing the disease to spread beyond the habitat of the original host mosquito.

4 Many infectious diseases originated in warm climates, where insects like mosquitoes live and thrive. As climate change leads to higher temperatures around the world, mosquitoes are now able to survive in areas that were once too cold for them. Figure 1 shows the range of *Aedes albopictus* and *Aedes aegypti*, both major vectors of tropical diseases, in the United States as of 2016. *Aedes aegypti*, once **confined** to tropical Africa, is expected to expand its range even farther with global warming.

5 The increasingly urban nature of the world's population also **facilitates** the **transmission** of disease. In large, crowded cities in developing countries, many people do not have regular household waste collection or access to clean drinking water. A household without running water is likely to catch and save rainwater in open containers, the perfect breeding ground[3] for mosquitoes, as are piles of trash and, above all, old tires.

6 Another aspect of urbanization contributing to the spread of pathogens is our close **proximity** to both wild and **domesticated** animals. Many dangerous pathogens have the ability to mutate and jump from one species to another, including to humans. Avian and swine flu are prime examples of such cross-species transfer, as is Ebola, which scientists believe originated among gorillas and chimpanzees. As various species experience the destruction of their habitats as a result of deforestation and urbanization, many are forced to live closer to human settlements, increasing the opportunity for the transmission of diseases from animals to humans. Domesticated animal populations are being squeezed as well. They are confined to increasingly crowded spaces, creating conditions that facilitate the transmission of disease.

7 Some pathogens, such as the ones that cause Ebola, are deadly, with no known cure. Others may not be as dangerous but still have an enormous economic impact in terms of lost productivity and the resources needed to fight them and provide healthcare for their victims. Some of these infectious diseases, once a local menace, now pose a global threat, and it will require a global effort to **eradicate** them.

[1]**pathogen** (n) a small organism that can cause disease
[2]**mutate** (v) to change genetically
[3]**breeding ground** (n) a place where organisms reproduce

Figure 1. The spread of *Aedes aegypti* and *Aedes albopictus* into the United States, as of 2016

Source: CDC

WHILE READING

3 Read the article. Which statement do you think the writer of the article would agree with?

    a Infectious diseases are a concern for people all over the world.
    b Scientists will soon find ways to prevent and treat these diseases.
    c Slowing global warming is the key to eradicating these diseases.
    d Most of these diseases are not likely to pose a threat to the United States in the near future.

4 Read the article again. Check (✔) the factors that contribute to the spread of infectious diseases as discussed in the article. Find four other factors that were discussed in the article and add them to the list.

    a climate change ☐
    b mutation of pathogens ☐
    c lack of access to healthcare ☐
    d global movement of populations ☐
    e drug resistance ☐
    f migration of vectors ☐
    g floods ☐

    1 _____
    2 _____
    3 _____
    4 _____

5 Use the phrases from the boxes to label the causal chains that start with urbanization.

> diseases spread more easily   mosquitoes breed freely
> no public water service   overcrowded cities
> people collect water

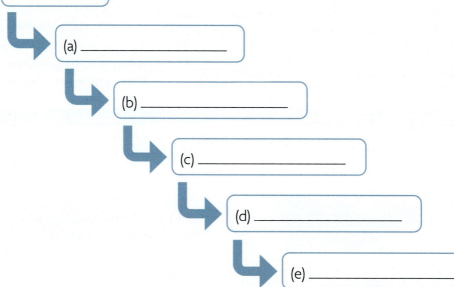

1 urbanization

(a) _____

(b) _____

(c) _____

(d) _____

(e) _____

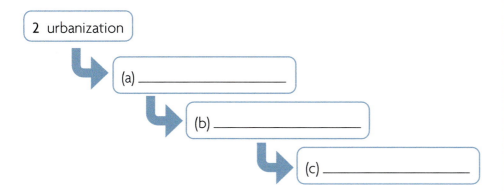

animals and humans live close together
disease is transmitted across species
habitat destruction

2 urbanization

(a) _____

(b) _____

(c) _____

READING BETWEEN THE LINES

6 Work with a partner. Complete the tasks.

MAKING INFERENCES

1 Reading 2 states, "In large, crowded cities in developing countries, many people do not have regular household waste collection or access to clean drinking water." This implies that some people do receive these services. Who do you think that is? Why?

2 Review Reading 2, paragraph 4 and Figure 1. The current most common vector for the chikungunya virus is *Aedes aegypti*. Complete the causal chain showing the potential spread of the virus in the United States.

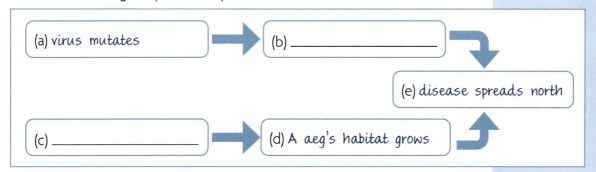

(a) virus mutates → (b) _____

(e) disease spreads north

(c) _____ → (d) A aeg's habitat grows

DISCUSSION

7 Work with a partner. Use ideas from Reading 1 and Reading 2 to discuss the questions.

SYNTHESIZING

1 Antibiotics are for bacterial infections. Antiviral drugs are for viruses. Sometimes, however, antibiotics are used as part of a larger treatment plan for viral diseases. What effect might this have on the increase in superbugs?

2 Both articles end by saying a global effort will be required to combat the spread of pathogens. What do you think can be done?

VERBS AND VERB PHRASES FOR CAUSATION

In order to write with precision, it is important to understand the differences in meaning among verbs and verb phrases that express aspects of causation.

Direct causation

Many diseases, such as malaria and chikungunya, **result from** the bite of a mosquito carrying the pathogen.

Part of a cause

Climate change **has contributed to** the spread of tropical diseases.

Makes effect easier to achieve

The poverty and crowded conditions in many modern cities **facilitate** the transmission of infectious diseases.

Passive causation

Global travel **allows** pathogens to spread more easily.

direct causation	part of cause	makes effect easier to achieve	passive causation
cause / be a cause of	be a factor	help	let*
lead to	contribute to	facilitate	allow
result in	affect	promote	permit
be a/the result of	impact	fuel	
create	influence	encourage	
trigger	have an effect on	foster	
produce	have a role in	enable	
bring about			
drive			

* Notice that, unlike other passive causation verbs, *let* is not followed by *to*:
*Global travel **lets** pathogens **spread** more easily.*

PRISM Digital Workbook

1 Complete the sentences with one of the verbs or verb phrases from the chart above. More than one answer is possible.

1 Health experts emphasize the importance of human behavior because our decisions can both _____ and prevent the spread of antibiotic-resistant superbugs.

2 Scientists have only recently begun to understand how climate change _____ the spread of vectors that carry infectious diseases.

3 Health officials are targeting containers of standing water that _____ mosquitoes to reproduce and spread disease.

4 A bacterial infection _____ an automatic response in which the body attempts to kill off the invading pathogens

5 Antibiotics often destroy only a percentage of the bacteria that cause infection, _____ the strongest to survive and even thrive.

2 Write two more sentences using expressions from the chart on page 170.

1 _____
_____

2 _____
_____

WORD FAMILIES

3 Complete the word families related to global health and medicine. Use a dictionary to help you if needed.

PRISM Digital Workbook

noun	verb	adjective	
access	(1)_____	(2)_____	
bacteria		(3)_____	
(4)_____	(5)_____	infectious	
(6)_____	mutate	mutant	
prevention	(7)_____	(8)_____	(9)_____
(10)_____	(11)_____	resistant	
therapy		(12)_____	
transmission	(13)_____	(14)_____	(15)_____
virus		(16)_____	

4 Complete the paragraph with words from Exercise 3 in the correct form.

The spread of infectious disease is a complex phenomenon. Health officials must deal with both (1)_____ and (2)_____ infections, caused by pathogens that can be (3)_____ from one host to another in different ways. What makes the situation even more challenging is that these pathogens can (4)_____ over time, allowing them to become (5)_____ to antibiotics. Once this occurs, these drugs are no longer (6)_____ , and scientists need find new ways to treat the infections. Many experts believe that a better option would be to develop a vaccine to (7)_____ these diseases from (8)_____ people in the first place.

WRITING

CRITICAL THINKING

At the end of this unit, you are going to write a cause-and-effect essay about factors that affect the spread of disease. Look at this unit's Writing Task below.

> Many infectious diseases that were once geographically limited now occur globally. Choose one disease and discuss the factors that may have contributed to its development and spread or could do so in the future.

SKILLS

Analyzing causes and effects

In academic writing it is important to be able to provide an analysis of why something happens and of the consequences of events, behavior, or decisions.

REMEMBER

1 Work with a partner. List the factors that you have read about in this unit that have contributed to the globalization of infection.

_____   _____
_____   _____
_____   _____
_____   _____
_____   _____

ANALYZE

2 Review these case histories for three infectious diseases that have created global concern in recent years. Go online and research another one. Prepare a case history for it in the space provided. With your partner, discuss the ways in which all the diseases are similar and how they differ.

Ⓐ chikungunya

- first documented cases in Tanzania in the 1950s
- spread through Africa and SE Asia
- first case in western hemisphere in 2013
- about 3 million infections/year
- rarely lethal—1 death per 1,000 infections
- symptoms include joint pain, headaches, fatigue, and may last for months or even years
- vectors: *Aedes aegypti* and more recently, *Aedes albopictus*
- crowded conditions needed to sustain transmission among humans
- virus
- no vaccine
- no specific treatment

B dengue

- frequent epidemics dating back to 17th century
- spread with migration of *Aedes aegypti,* which accompanied slave trade
- 1/3 of global population now at risk
- 50–100 million infections annually
- 22,000 deaths annually
- vectors: *Aedes aegypti* and more recently, *Aedes albopictus*
- crowded conditions needed to sustain transmission among humans
- symptoms include rash, fever, headaches, joint pain
- virus
- vaccine in development
- no specific treatment

C Zika virus

- first identified in monkeys in 1947 in Uganda
- first human infection in 1952
- spread through Africa and Asia in 1950s–1980s
- crossed Pacific and arrived in western hemisphere in 2015
- many of those infected have no symptoms, so it is difficult to estimate the rate of infection
- 4 million annual infections are projected
- most cases are mild, but it can cause birth defects if mother is infected
- vectors: primarily *Aedes aegypti*
- crowded conditions needed to sustain transmission among humans
- vaccine in development
- no specific treatment

D _____

- _____
- _____
- _____
- _____
- _____
- _____
- _____
- _____
- _____
- _____

3 Review your list of factors from Exercise 1. For each of the infectious diseases in Exercise 2, write down the three factors that have contributed most to their development and spread or will do so in the future.

chikungunya	dengue	Zika virus	_____

4 Work with a partner. Read the facts about chikungunya and dengue. Then list some possible consequences of the spread of these diseases.

Facts:
- Most people who contract these diseases remain ill for 1–2 weeks. They cannot work or attend school during that period.
- Although there is no known cure, many patients seek a doctor's care for relief of the symptoms.
- Some patients, especially young children, require hospitalization.
- A small percentage of cases are fatal.

Consequences:
For individuals and families:

_____

_____

_____

For nations and regions:

_____

_____

_____

GRAMMAR FOR WRITING

CAUSE AND EFFECT: LOGICAL CONNECTORS

There are many different ways to express causes, reasons, effects, and consequences using logical connectors.

to connect a noun phrase and an independent clause

as a result of [cause]
because of [reason]
due to [cause]
thanks to [cause]

to connect a dependent and an independent clause

because [reason]
since [reason]
[reason] *so that*

to connect two independent clauses

as a result [effect]
as a consequence [effect]
consequently [effect]
therefore [effect]
so [effect]

Some verbs, nouns, and connectors look and sound similar, so they are easy to confuse. Take care when using these logical connectors.

because / because of

Because the earth is getting warmer, the habitat of some mosquitoes is growing.
Some experts believe superbugs have emerged **because of** the misuse of antibiotics.

as a consequence / is a consequence of

Some of the bacteria survive; **as a consequence**, the bacteria become drug-resistant.
Often, drug resistance **is a consequence of** the misuse of antibiotics.

as a result / results in / results from

Some of the bacteria survive; **as a result**, the bacteria become drug-resistant.
Long-term illness **results in** a loss of productivity for families and entire nations.
Birth defects may **result from** a mother's exposure to the virus during pregnancy.

1 Review the table in Critical Thinking, Exercise 3. Write three sentences about factors in the globalization of infection. Use logical connectors.

1 _____

2 _____

3 _____

2 Review Critical Thinking, Exercise 4. Write two sentences describing the consequences of the spread of infectious diseases. Use logical connectors.

1 _____

2 _____

PRISM Digital Workbook

SKILLS

Writing about causes and effects

Academic writing often includes explanations for why something happens or the consequences of events, behavior, or decisions. The first involves an analysis of causes, whereas the second requires an analysis of effects.

- A causal analysis addresses causal factors in a situation or decision.
- An effect analysis addresses the consequences of an event or situation.

These analyses may be chains; in other words, one cause may lead to an effect that causes another effect. The distinction between causes and effects is not always clear cut, as the effect of one situation can become the cause of another, and so on.

More complex pieces of writing may include both types of analysis.

PRISM | Digital Workbook

1 Review the articles in this unit. Do they involve primarily an analysis of causes or effects?

a Reading 1 _____   **b** Reading 2 _____

2 Work with a partner. Complete the tasks, first following the examples (items 1–3), then on your own (items 4–6).

   1 Climate change is primarily the result of human activity. It is having a serious impact on the Arctic. Review this list of the effects of climate change.
   - Glaciers are melting: getting weaker and smaller.
   - There's an increase in shipping and other commercial activities.
   - Floating ice, an important habitat for polar animals, is disappearing.
   - Arctic areas are more accessible to humans.
   - Sea ice is melting.
   - Strong Arctic storms are more frequent.
   - Arctic animals, such as polar bears, have become endangered.
   - The ocean is getting warmer.
   - Storms are breaking up weak areas of glaciers.

   2 Study this chain based on the information in Task 1 above. Develop another cause or effect chain using at least three of the facts from Task 1.

3 Write a short paragraph describing the cause-and-effect relationships in your chain in Task 2. Use the words, phrases, and grammatical structures of cause and effect that you have learned in this unit.

> Higher ocean temperatures have had a dramatic impact in the Arctic, and not everyone thinks this is negative. The warmer climate has weakened the glaciers, making them vulnerable to increasingly frequent storms, which are also fueled by the warmer water. As a consequence, Arctic areas, almost impossible to navigate in the past, are suddenly more accessible to shipping and commercial operations.

4 People leave their countries and immigrate to other countries for many different reasons. Review this list of factors that might affect someone's decision to leave. Add any others you can think of.
   - The economy is weak.
   - There is no freedom of religion.
   - The government is repressive.
   - There is high unemployment.
   - Government services (health, education, etc.) are poor.
   - There is no freedom of speech.
   - The government has put people in jail for political activities.
   - There is political unrest.
   - There is a lot of crime. The streets are dangerous.
   - It is difficult for children to get a good education.
5 Develop two causal chains, each utilizing at least three of the factors from Task 4.
6 Each of you take one of the causal chains you created in Task 5 and write a short paragraph describing the cause-and-effect relationships in the chain. Use the words, phrases, and grammatical structures of cause and effect that you have learned in this unit. Review each other's paragraphs.

_____
_____
_____
_____
_____
_____
_____
_____
_____
_____

WRITING TASK

Many infectious diseases that were once geographically limited now occur globally. Choose one disease and discuss the factors that may have contributed to its development and spread or could do so in the future.

PLAN

1 Develop two or three causal chains for the disease you are writing about. (Review Critical Thinking, Exercise 3.) These will be the basis of your body paragraphs.

2 For each of your causal chains, write a topic sentence that introduces and unites the material in that chain. (Review Academic Writing Skills, Exercise 2.)

_____

_____

_____

_____

_____

_____

3 Think about the introductory paragraph.

   1 What background information could you include? Review the cards in Critical Thinking, Exercise 2, and highlight possible points to include.
   2 What claim will you make about the spread of this disease?

   _____

   3 Write a thesis statement that expresses the claim.

   _____

   _____

   _____

4 Think about your conclusion.

   1 How will you begin your conclusion? Be sure to remind your readers of the importance of your claim, but do not repeat your thesis statement.
   2 What do you want your readers to think about as they finish your essay?

   future possibilities ☐
   wider consequences ☐
   implications ☐
   other: _____

5 Refer to the Task Checklist on page 179 as you prepare your essay.

WRITE A FIRST DRAFT

6 Write your cause-and-effect essay based on your essay plan. Write 500–600 words.

REVISE

7 Use the Task Checklist to review your essay for content and structure.

TASK CHECKLIST	✔
Have you introduced and provided background on the infectious disease?	
Have you stated your claim clearly in your thesis statement?	
Have you developed and explained the causal chains in the spread of the disease?	
Does each body paragraph provide evidence to support your claim?	
Does each paragraph have a topic sentence that unifies all of the material in the paragraph?	
Is there a concluding paragraph that refers to your claim and leaves the reader with something to think about?	

8 Make any necessary changes to your essay.

EDIT

9 Use the Language Checklist to edit your essay for language errors.

LANGUAGE CHECKLIST	✔
When discussing causation, did you use the verbs and verbal phrases you learned about in this unit?	
Did you use the correct form for global health words?	
Did you use logical connectors correctly?	

10 Make any necessary changes to your essay.

ON CAMPUS

APPLYING TO A DEGREE PROGRAM

Writing an application to a degree program takes time and careful thought. The essay is often the most challenging part of the application. It is also one of the most important because it shows admissions officers who you are.

PREPARING TO READ

1 Work with a partner. Most colleges require applicants to write an essay. What sorts of topics and information do you think a student should include in an application essay? What should be avoided?

WHILE READING

2 Read the guidelines for writing an essay for a college application on the next page. Then indicate whether each statement below is good advice (*G*) or bad advice (*B*).

1 Use a dictionary or thesaurus for richer vocabulary in your essay. _____
2 Write a long essay because it is more impressive. _____
3 Revise your essay after you get feedback from a friend. _____
4 Describe the one-week field trip you once took as an internship. _____
5 Explain what you learned from being a team leader. _____
6 Mention something related to your subject that was recently in the news. _____

PRACTICE

3 Work with a partner. Which of these sentences should be included in an application essay? Explain your choices to another pair.

1 It is my dream to attend the Sinclair University, one of the finest colleges in the country with excellent faculty and outstanding programs. ☐
2 My desire to study nursing became clear when I volunteered at a local hospital and cared for children with long-term illnesses. ☐
3 Though we did not win the robotics competition, we worked together really well and we designed something we were proud of. ☐
4 I want to find meaningful work that will make the world a better place. ☐
5 It was the first time I worked with someone who was deaf, and it changed the way I thought about human communication. ☐
6 We camped next to an active volcano. It was totally awesome! ☐

All applicants are asked to submit an essay that is no more than 1,000 words. Applicants to graduate programs must submit a Statement of Purpose. Undergraduate applicants are asked for a Personal Statement.

Statement of Purpose

This essay focuses on your educational and career background and your goals.

Include:

- specific educational and career goals.
- how this program, faculty, or university will help you achieve your goals.
- relevant courses you have taken.
- experiences that have prepared you for your studies.
- information that shows your knowledge of current issues in your field.

Don't include:

- anything from high school or earlier.
- experiences or skills that aren't relevant to your studies.
- exaggerations of your accomplishments.

Personal Statement

This essay should show us what kind of person you are.

Include:

- an answer to the essay question.
- why you chose your major.
- personal stories that show positive qualities, like resilience[1] or initiative[2].
- what you have learned from your experiences.
- skills that transfer from one situation to another, like teamwork or organization.

Don't include:

- big words that you really don't know.
- sentences that are not original or meaningful, such as *I have always wanted to be a teacher* or *This college will provide a good education for my future.*

General tips for all application essays

DO:

- check your essay for spelling, grammar, and punctuation.
- ask someone to proofread and give feedback on the content of your essay.
- expect to write several drafts.

DON'T:

- go over the word limit.
- use flattery[3] in your essay.
- use contractions, like *can't* or *isn't*.
- use uncommon abbreviations.
- use slang or unprofessional language.

[1]**resilience** (n) the ability to recover quickly from a difficult situation
[2]**initiative** (n) the drive to start new things
[3]**flattery** (n) excessive compliments that are often insincere

REAL-WORLD APPLICATION

4 Research a college or university to find out about its essay requirement. Write an appropriate application essay. Then work with a partner to review and revise your essays.

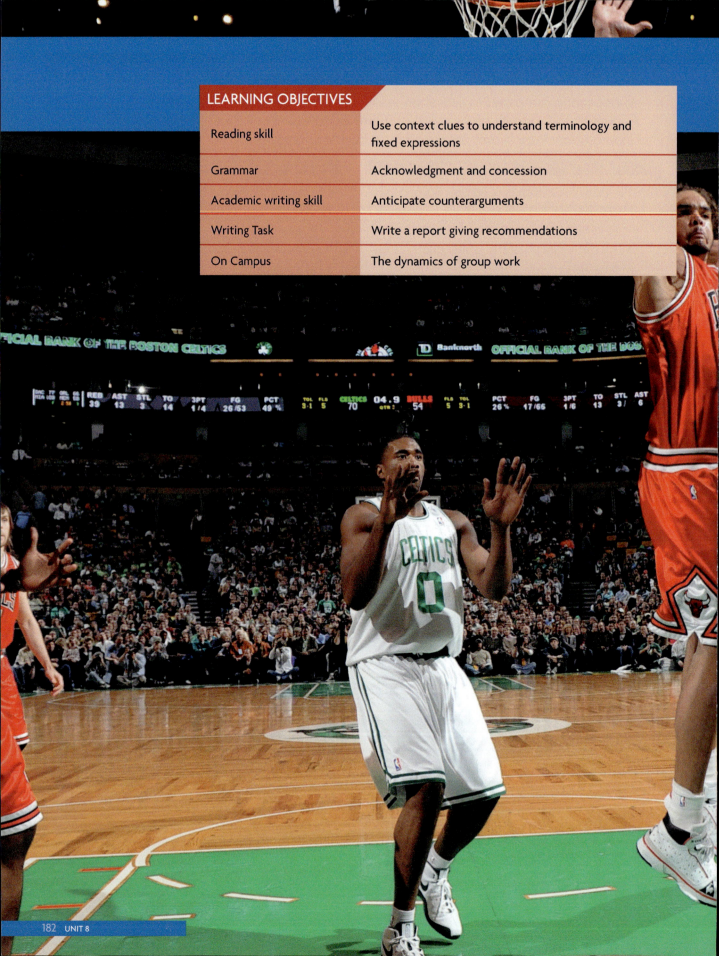

LEARNING OBJECTIVES

Reading skill	Use context clues to understand terminology and fixed expressions
Grammar	Acknowledgment and concession
Academic writing skill	Anticipate counterarguments
Writing Task	Write a report giving recommendations
On Campus	The dynamics of group work

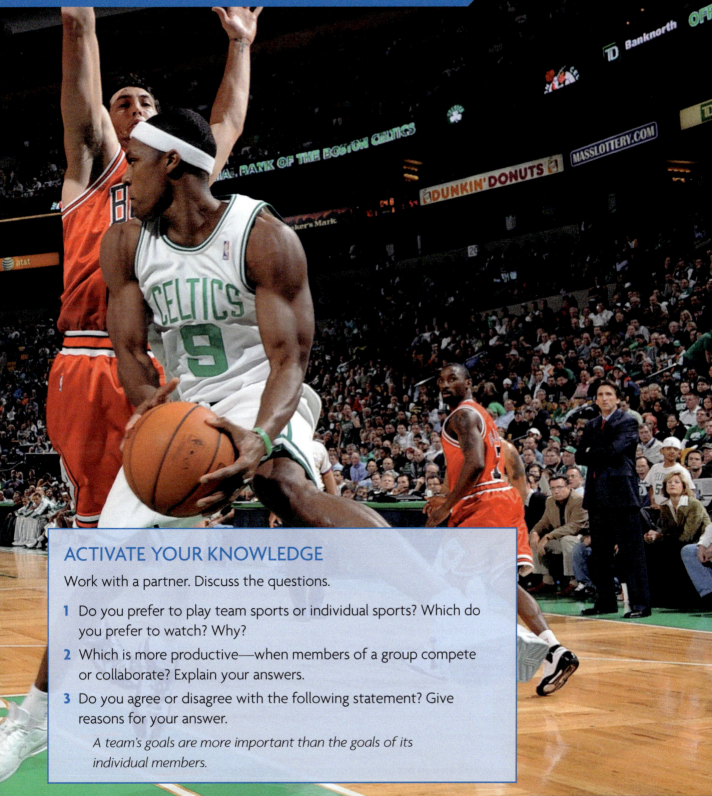

COLLABORATION

ACTIVATE YOUR KNOWLEDGE

Work with a partner. Discuss the questions.

1 Do you prefer to play team sports or individual sports? Which do you prefer to watch? Why?

2 Which is more productive—when members of a group compete or collaborate? Explain your answers.

3 Do you agree or disagree with the following statement? Give reasons for your answer.

A team's goals are more important than the goals of its individual members.

WATCH AND LISTEN

PREPARING TO WATCH

ACTIVATING YOUR
KNOWLEDGE

1 Check (✔) the ideas you agree with. Discuss your choices with a partner.

1 I prefer to work alone. ☐
2 I prefer to work with others. ☐
3 I like working in a quiet office environment. ☐
4 I like working in an open space where I can hear others. ☐
5 I would like to work for a company that encourages play. ☐
6 I would like to work for a company that is flexible. ☐

PREDICTING CONTENT
USING VISUALS

2 Look at the pictures from the video. Discuss the questions with your partner.

1 Does the workspace in the first picture look like a typical office? Why or why not?
2 What are the advantages of working in open spaces? What are the disadvantages?
3 What things would you like to have at your workplace, now or someday—basketball courts? Table tennis? Meditation gardens?
4 Do you think pets should be allowed in offices? Why or why not? What are some of the advantages and disadvantages of bringing your pet to work with you?

GLOSSARY

indelible (adj) impossible to remove by washing or any other method

mindset (n) a person's way of thinking and their opinions

congregate (v) to gather together into a large group

communal (adj) belonging to or used by all members of a group

synergy (n) the combined power of a group of things when they are working together that is greater than the total power achieved by each working separately

pull (v, informal) to do or accomplish something, such as an extended period of work

all-nighter (n) a time when you spend all night working on something

one-upmanship (n) an effort to show that you are better than someone you are competing with

rule with an iron fist (idm) to control a group of people very firmly, having complete power over everything they do

WHILE WATCHING

3 ▶ Watch the video. Circle the correct answer.

1 What does the informal workspace reduce?
  a collaboration
  b seriousness
  c the need to meet people

2 Which of the following is **not** common at this creative company?
  a working over a hundred hours a week
  b synergy between people
  c scheduling a place to get work done

3 What does the president, Carisa Bianci, believe this type of workspace encourages?
  a an employee's best performance
  b competition from other companies
  c relaxation

4 ▶ Watch the video again. Write details for each main idea.

1 Communities are organized within the spaces.
  _____
  _____

2 Communal spaces serve several functions.
  _____
  _____

3 Healthy competition exists within the building.
  _____
  _____

4 The office design also provides places where people can be alone and work independently.
  _____
  _____

5 Work with a partner. Discuss the questions.

1 How do you think the employees feel about the space?
2 Why do you think playing basketball is encouraged?
3 Why do you think employees sometimes work over 100 hours a week?

DISCUSSION

6 Discuss the questions with your partner.

1 Would you like to work at a creative company like the one in the video? Why or why not?
2 Does increased collaboration always benefit a company? Why or why not?
3 Why do you think more and more offices are changing their culture?

READING

READING 1

PREPARING TO READ

1 You are going to read an article about the value of talented individuals within teams. Work with a partner. Read the first sentence of each paragraph in the reading on pages 187–188. Then discuss the questions.

1 What broader lessons do you think we can learn from sports teams?
2 What do you think chickens have to do with sports?
3 How important is the talent of individual players to a team's success?

2 Read the definitions. Complete the sentences with the correct form of the words in bold.

> **accomplish** (v) to do something successfully
> **coordinate** (v) to make separate things or people work well together
> **decline** (v) to worsen; to decrease
> **detract from** (v) to make something worse or less valuable
> **differentiate** (v) to show or find the difference between one thing and another
> **enhance** (v) to improve
> **isolate** (v) to separate something from other connected things
> **phenomenon** (n) something that can be experienced or felt, especially something that is unusual or new

1 The soft colors and elegant furniture _____ the restaurant's appearance.
2 We can't work independently. We'll need to _____ our efforts if we want this project to be a success.
3 Sales have _____ since the government increased taxes on consumer goods.
4 We have _____ a lot in the last five years, but we still have more work to do in order to reach our goals.
5 El Niño is a _____ that brings unpredictable and unusual weather to many parts of the world.
6 The bright colors of the male bird's feathers _____ it from the female.
7 Cans, bottles, and other garbage _____ the natural beauty of the beach.
8 Doctors have been unable to _____ the cause of the patient's fever, so they are doing more tests.

WHILE READING

3 Read the article. Highlight the sentences that express the main ideas. Highlight only key points—no more than five sentences.

READING FOR
MAIN IDEAS

SUMMARIZING

4 Complete the summary. Then compare work with a partner.

> Some sports teams are a lot like chickens. Too many high-level individual performers (1)_____ from the (2)_____ of the group. This is most likely to happen in sports such as soccer and (3)_____ , in which team members need to (4)_____ their actions. Star athletes, like star chickens, may be more likely to (5)_____ their own goals than work for the group's best interests.

5 Scan the article to find these terms. Explain them in your own words.

READING FOR DETAILS

a task interdependence _____

b the Ringelmann effect _____

THE VALUE OF TALENT

1 Much of the work in today's world is **accomplished** in teams: in business, in scientific research, in government, on movie sets, and of course, in sports. Most people believe that the best way to build a great team is to assemble a group of the best, most talented individuals. Facebook's Mark Zuckerberg, commenting on the value of talent, is quoted as saying that one great engineer is worth a hundred average ones. And Zuckerberg is certainly someone who knows how to build an A-team.

2 Animal scientist William Muir wondered if he could build such an A-team—with chickens. He looked for the most productive egg producers and bred[1] them for six generations. This was his test group. For comparison, he did the same thing with a selection of average egg producers. This was his control group. To his surprise, six generations later, he found that the egg production of the test group was lower than that of the control group. He discovered that the super-producers in the test group used an enormous amount of energy constantly re-establishing a pecking order, keeping themselves at the top. As a result, they had little energy left for egg production.

3 Of course, chickens are not a team, but this kind of group interaction and its effect on production piqued the interest of researchers who study teams and teamwork. The owners of sports teams spend millions of dollars to attract top talent[2]. Companies spend millions to hire top businesspeople. They want to know if their money is well spent.

4 A recent series of studies examined the role of talent in the sports world. They focused on three different sports: World Cup soccer, professional basketball, and professional baseball. The results were mixed. For soccer and basketball, the studies revealed that adding talented players to a team is indeed a good strategy, but only up to a point. Performance peaked when about 70% of the players were considered top talent; above that level, the team's performance began to **decline**. Interestingly, this trend was not evident in baseball, where additional individual talent continued to **enhance** the team's performance *(Figures 1 and 2)*.

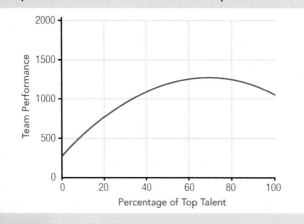

Figure 1. Team performance as a function of top talent on the team: World Cup Soccer

Source: Swaab et al, 2014

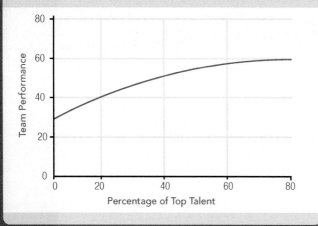

Figure 2. Team performance as a function of top talent on the team: Major League Baseball

Source: Swaab et al, 2014

5 In looking for an explanation for the different results for different sports, the researchers **isolated** one important factor—the extent to which a good performance by a team requires its members to **coordinate** their actions. This *task interdependence* **differentiates** baseball from basketball and soccer.

In baseball, the performance of individual players is less dependent on teammates than in soccer and basketball. The researchers concluded that when, during the course of play, task interdependence is high, team performance will suffer when there is too much talent in the group. When task interdependence is lower, on the other hand, individual talent will have a positive effect on team performance.

6 One explanation for this **phenomenon** is not so far from the pecking order situation among chickens. If a basketball star is pursuing his own personal goals, for example, trying to amass a high personal point total, he may be less generous as a team player. He may take a shot himself when it would be better to pass the ball to a teammate, **detracting from** the team's overall performance. Young children learning to play team sports are often told, "There is no *I* in *TEAM*." Stars apparently do not follow this basic principle of sportsmanship.

7 Another possibility is that when there is a lot of talent on a team, some players may begin to make less effort. This is referred to as the *Ringelmann effect*. Maximilien Ringelmann, a French agricultural engineer, conducted an experiment in 1913 in which he asked two, three, four, and up to 28 people to participate in a game of tug-of-war. He measured how much force each person used to pull the rope. He found that whenever he added a person to the team, everyone else pulled with less force.

8 Assembling the ideal team—for sports, business, science, or entertainment—is more complicated than simply hiring the best talent. An A-team may require a balance—not just A players, but a few generous B players as well.

---

[1]**bred** (v; past and past participle of *breed*) for animals and plants, managed and controlled the reproduction of
[2]**talent** (n) especially in sports and entertainment, a collective term for the people possessing notable talent

READING BETWEEN THE LINES

SKILLS

Using context clues to understand terminology

Formal writing often contains topic-specific terminology and expressions as well as higher-level vocabulary that readers may not know. Elements of context can help you determine the meaning of unfamiliar terms. Here are some context clues to look for.

Cultural or world knowledge

*Before the games, athletes carry the Olympic **torch** to cities around the host country.*

Everyone is familiar with the tradition of athletes carrying the symbol of the Games, the Olympic flame, so you can guess the meaning of *torch*.

Components of multiword expressions or parts of words

*Recent trade figures are evidence of the **interdependence** of the two countries.*

You already know the meaning of the two parts, *inter + dependence*, so you can guess the meaning of the term.

Contrast

*The committee rejected the job candidate. He didn't seem very energetic, and they were looking for someone more **dynamic**.*

So someone who is dynamic is the opposite of someone with low energy.

Examples

***Typhoons**, such as the devastating storm Haiyan in the Philippines in 2013, can cause considerable damage.*

If you are familiar with the storm named Haiyan, you can guess the meaning of *typhoon*.

Logical inference

*Scientists **bred** chickens for six generations to examine their behavior over time.*

If you consider what scientists could do to chickens for six generations with the purpose of understanding their behavior, you can guess the meaning of *bred*.

---

6 Work with a partner. Use context clues to discuss the possible meaning of these terms from Reading 1.

1 **A-team** (para 1): What does the term mean? Is it limited to sports?
2 **pecking order** (para 2): Chickens peck one another to show dominance. How could this relate to teams in different contexts?
3 **tug-of-war** (para 7): Read the paragraph and describe what you think happens in this game. Do an image search to check your ideas. How might this term be used in other contexts?

WORKING OUT MEANING

DISCUSSION

7 In small groups, take turns describing an experience that you have had working in a group, such as a music group, a class or volunteer project, or some other context. Include answers to these questions.

1 Was it a positive or negative experience?
2 What factors do you think contributed to the group's success or lack of success?
3 Explain the meaning of the expression "There is no *I* in *TEAM*." Do you think it is a good message? Why or why not?

READING 2

PREPARING TO READ

USING YOUR KNOWLEDGE

1 You are going to read an article about group intelligence. Look at these statements. Do you think they are true or false? Write *T* (true) or *F* (false).

_____ 1 The intelligence of a group is equal to the intelligence of its members added together.

_____ 2 People who have similar interests and backgrounds work together better than people who are very different.

_____ 3 You can tell a lot about how well people are communicating by just looking at their facial expressions.

_____ 4 Communication works best when people believe that others will respect what they say.

_____ 5 In a meeting, it is a waste of time for people to talk to each other instead of listening to the leader.

_____ 6 People can communicate just as effectively using technology (IM, email, teleconferencing) as they can meeting face to face.

2 After you have finished reading, come back and check your answers.

3 Read the sentences and write the words in bold next to the definitions.

1 He held his fists high in the air, a **gesture** that made it very clear how excited he was.

2 If you want to be well prepared for the test, you should study in a quiet place that has no **distractions**—not even a window or a television.

3 Scientists believe that genetic mutations **underlie** a wide range of diseases and disorders.

4 Children who **display** aggressive or angry behavior in school may be having problems at home.

5 She said she would be arriving late. **Apparently**, a lot of flights have been delayed because of bad weather.

6 One of the **fundamental** principles of democracy is the freedom to express one's opinion freely.

7 The student's performance has been very **consistent**. She gets about 80% on most assignments and tests.

8 This study focuses **exclusively** on the behavior of children. Adults behave very differently and were investigated in a separate study.

a _____ (adj) basic, being the thing on which other things depend

b _____ (adv) limited to a specific thing, person, or group

c _____ (v) to be the cause of or a strong influence on something

d _____ (n) a movement of the body or a body part to express an idea or feeling

e _____ (n) something that prevents someone from giving full attention to something else

f _____ (adj) always behaving or happening in the same way

g _____ (adv) according to what seems to be true

h _____ (v) to show a feeling or attitude by what you say or do

WHILE READING

4 Read the article on page 192. Highlight the sentences that best express the main ideas of the article. Highlight no more than six sentences.

5 Write a summary of the article using your highlighting to guide you. Read another student's paragraph and offer each other advice for improvement.

_____

_____

_____

_____

_____

_____

_____

READING FOR MAIN IDEAS

SUMMARIZING

THE PERFECT WORK TEAM

1 For years, psychologists have known how to measure the intelligence of individuals, but only recently have they begun to investigate the issue of *group intelligence*. This notion stems from the observation that some groups seem to work well across tasks, even tasks that are not very similar. Early investigations suggest that group intelligence is not the sum of the intelligence of the individuals in it. So what is the secret to their success?

2 Researchers at Google and MIT have both tackled this question and they believe they finally have a handle on what makes some teams successful. In the Google study, researchers amassed thousands of data points on hundreds of groups and combed through them trying to find patterns. Are the members of effective groups friends outside of work? Do groups whose members have similar personalities or backgrounds work together best? Does gender make a difference? They floated many theories but found no patterns to support them. In fact, *who* was in the group **apparently** did not seem to make a difference; instead, the difference between more and less effective groups seemed to lie in the interaction among the members.

3 The MIT group had already been gathering data on group interaction using digital "badges" that participants in the study agreed to wear. These badges provided a wealth of information, including how long people spoke and to whom, what kinds of **gestures** they made, where they were looking during interaction, and their facial expressions. As in the Google study, this research group concluded that the key to an effective team is how members interact.

4 Among the findings, the most **consistent** and significant is that, in effective groups, members spoke for a roughly equal amount of time—not at every meeting or interaction, but across the course of a project. A second consistent finding was that members **displayed** empathy, an understanding of how it might feel to walk in someone else's shoes. This social sensitivity is measured by a relatively new test, called the "Reading the Mind in the Eyes." The test assesses individual differences in two key factors, social awareness and emotion recognition, by asking individuals to guess emotions based on only a picture of a person's eyes. A high level of these two features create what one of the researchers in the Google study calls *psychological safety*: Members of the group feel comfortable voicing their opinions and making suggestions without fear of a negative response from other members of the group, and they believe that others will listen to them and value what they say. When these conditions are present, the group as a whole tends to be effective.

5 There were additional findings that support these general ones. For example, in effective groups, members face one another directly when they speak, they use energetic and enthusiastic gestures. They also communicate directly with one another, not just through the leader or manager of the group. In fact, the MIT study found that side conversations between individual members during meetings, far from being a **distraction**, actually increased the group's productivity. All the findings highlight the importance of having face-to-face meetings instead of phone calls, teleconferences, or communicating by email. The positive behaviors uncovered in these studies occur primarily or **exclusively** in face-to-face interaction. The MIT team estimates that 35% of a team's performance can be explained just by the number of their face-to-face exchanges.

6 One might argue that most of these findings are extremely obvious, and needless to say, good managers have probably always understood these principles. Our social and professional lives, however, are not always structured in ways that facilitate the kind of interaction that apparently **underlies** effective group performance. Understanding group intelligence can help businesses and other organizations make the **fundamental** changes necessary to improve group performance.

6 Read the article again. Complete the table with results from the MIT study about the characteristics of effective groups and their members.

major findings	1 *equal speaking time*
	2
additional findings	3
	4 *gestures*
	5
	6

7 Scan Reading 2 to find these terms. Explain each of them in your own words.

a group intelligence _____

b psychological safety _____

READING BETWEEN THE LINES

SKILLS

Using context clues to understand fixed expressions

You can use some of the same techniques described on page 189 to determine the meaning of idioms and other fixed expressions.

With idioms, sometimes understanding each word can help you understand the whole meaning, but often the meaning is not clearly related to its components. In those cases, you will need to use a more global approach, such as logical inference.

8 Work with a partner. Use context clues to work out the meaning of these expressions. Paragraph numbers are given in parentheses.

1 have a handle on (para 2): _____

2 walk in someone else's shoes (para 4): _____

3 needless to say (para 6): _____

PRISM **Digital** Workbook

DISCUSSION

9 Work in small groups to do a version of the test mentioned in Reading 2.

    1 Look carefully but quickly at each set of eyes.

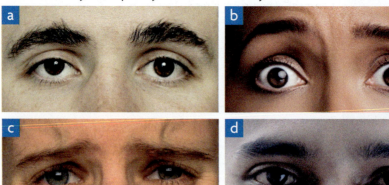

    2 Choose the word that you think best describes how the person is feeling.

    3 Compare your choices with those of the others in your group. Discuss the reasons for your choices.

⊙ LANGUAGE DEVELOPMENT

LANGUAGE FOR HEDGING

In some forms of writing it is fine to make bold, unqualified claims and generalizations. In formal writing, however, writers need to make it clear that they understand that other viewpoints exist and have credibility. Formal writers do not often take absolute positions. Instead, they limit generalizations and hedge their claims to make them more modest—and as protection from accusations that their work is untrue or misleading.

Bold claim

Face-to-face interaction is the most effective form of communication.

Hedged claim

In most cases, face-to-face interaction is the most effective form of communication.

It has been suggested that face-to-face interaction is the most effective form of communication.

Face-to-face interaction **may/tends to** be the most effective form of communication.

Hedging devices

There are many ways to hedge or soften a claim.

Quantifiers and approximators
most / some / many
fairly / somewhat
often / usually
more or less

Adverbs and adverb phrases
for the most part
primarily
apparently
relatively
perhaps
typically
mainly
generally
in general

Modal verbs
can / could / may

Lexical verbs and phrases
tends
suggests
seems
appears
is likely to

Introductory phrases
There is evidence that
It appears / seems that
It has been suggested that
This indicates that
It may be the case that
It is (often) thought that
It is widely believed / assumed that

1 Rewrite these bold claims to make them more modest. Compare sentences with a partner.

1 Human error is the cause of traffic fatalities.

_____

2 Lack of sleep leads to both emotional and physical problems.

_____

3 If you know your personality type, you can find the job that is best for you.

_____

4 Tall people make the best basketball players.

_____

5 People who are obese will develop diabetes.

_____

6 We will run out of fossil fuels in about 100 years.

_____

2 Write three hedged statements of your own about building teams for effective collaboration.

1 _____
2 _____
3 _____

WRITING

CRITICAL THINKING

At the end of this unit, you will write a report on how to assemble an effective team for a particular organization. Look at this unit's Writing Task below.

> Applying the principles you have learned in this unit, present your recommendations for assembling and organizing an effective team for a particular business or collaborative group.

Understanding audience and purpose

Writers write for a purpose: to inform, entertain, instruct, or persuade. Most of the time, they also write for a particular audience. A report to a group of business professionals will be different from an academic essay for a professor. It is important to keep both purpose and audience in mind whenever you write.

 UNDERSTAND

1 Review the information about four different organizations who want your advice about team building. Write one noun phrase to describe each team you will be helping to build (e.g., *a team of top lawyers for a high-profile court case*).

1 _____

2 _____

3 _____

4 _____

Investment bank
- *Rockethedge* is a top Wall Street firm that hires graduates of the best business schools all over the world.
- Employees are expected to work long hours, but they receive extremely high salaries.
- The firm makes money by billing its clients for services. Employees are successful if their billing level is high. If their level drops, they are likely to be fired.
- The firm is launching a new division that will concentrate on start-up companies. The new division will be staffed by current and newly hired employees and will report to the president of the company. Your report is to focus on this new division.

Professional soccer team

- Saxton, California, plans to field a professional soccer team, the *Chupacabras*. City officials believe it will increase the appeal of the city and attract new residents and visitors.
- The city has set aside a significant amount of money to build the team, but the budget has limits. The city needs to spend the money wisely.
- A researcher has assembled a list of current professional players' records as well as information on college players who are about to graduate.
- The city has nine months to recruit and train the players for next year's season.

High-tech company that analyzes data and develops mathematical models

- Cybergogo is a relatively new company—it began as a start-up three years ago.
- Almost all of the employees are young—under 35—and most of them telecommute. They work at home, from coffee shops, or while they are traveling anywhere in the world.
- The company is bidding for a big job for a major international food service company. They have to prepare a proposal in the next six weeks based on requirements that the food service company has provided.
- The last time Cybergogo bid for a similar job, they did not get the contract, in part because they did not complete the proposal on time.

University track team

- Smythe University has always had a powerful track team. Recently, however, their record has been poor.
- Most of the money the university gets from fundraising, especially from former students, depends on the success of the team.
- The president of the university wants to rebuild the team. He is willing to spend as much money as necessary on scholarships for talented students, new staff hiring, and equipment upgrades to build a winning team.
- The president wants to concentrate on short-distance running and jumping events.

2 Work in small groups of three or four. Make a list of each organization's goals and the challenges you think it faces in meeting those goals. If the organization has experienced problems in the past, list these among the challenges.

organization	goal(s)	challenges
Rockethedge		
Saxton, California		
Cybergogo		
Smythe University		

3 Work in your group. Complete the task.

You have learned that there is an interaction effect between the kind of people on the team and the types of tasks they need to perform.

1 Think about the tasks that each of the organizations has to perform.
2 For the organizations that do not yet have members, make some notes on what kinds of team members, or combination of different kinds of team members, you think would be most effective.
3 For the organizations that already have members, make notes about any changes you would recommend.

4 Work in your group. Complete the task.

You have learned that on effective teams, members engage in very specific behaviors.

1 Brainstorm a list of effective behaviors.
2 Based on your ideas, for each of the four organizations, write down the three most important things you would include in your report. Look back at the list of challenges you made in Exercise 2. Could your recommendations help overcome some of these challenges?

GRAMMAR FOR WRITING

ACKNOWLEDGMENT AND CONCESSION

In writing a formal report, writers often need to acknowledge the validity of alternate perspectives as well as provide support for their own, often opposing, claim.

This usually follows a standard pattern:

1 Concession:
   a state the alternate perspective
   b say why it might be considered valid (this part may be omitted)

2 Support: show why it is, in fact, **not** valid, by providing support for your claim.

It is widely believed that eyewitnesses can provide reliable reports, and there is no
                                              (1a)

doubt that they can provide valuable information. However, research **suggests** their
                    (1b)   (2)

reports are not always entirely accurate.

Notice that both the concession and the claim contain hedged language (**bold** text).

Concession is generally indicated by one of many different logical connectors:

to connect a noun phrase and an independent clause	to connect a dependent and independent clause	to connect two independent clauses
despite	although	but
in spite of	even though	however
	whereas	nevertheless
	while	yet

1 Work with a partner. Read the statements. None of them is entirely true. Brainstorm ideas about why people may believe they are true, and think of possible support for the counterargument.

   1 Too much sugar makes children behave badly.
   2 Coffee makes you thirsty.
   3 Antibiotics will help you get better more quickly.

2 Now write a claim with a concession statement for each of the assertions in Exercise 1. Make sure each of your sentences includes the following:

   • a concession
   • a logical connector that indicates concession
   • a claim
   • hedged language

PRISM Digital Workbook

SKILLS

Anticipating counterarguments

In formal writing, good writers must anticipate, explore, acknowledge, and often counter objections or other points of view. This generally requires more than a single concession statement. They begin by exploring the other point of view and then provide evidence against it. Then they build support for their own claim.

PRISM **Digital** Workbook

1 Expand two of your sentences from Grammar for Writing, Exercise 1, into paragraphs, using the additional information provided below.

Eyewitnesses often have partial or inaccurate memories.

> It is widely believed that eyewitnesses can provide reliable reports, and there is no doubt that they can provide valuable information. These statements are an important building block in many criminal cases. However, research suggests that their reports are not always entirely accurate. In fact, an eyewitness report usually reflects a partial and often inaccurate memory of events as they happened. For this reason, we should not depend on them too heavily.

1 Sugar does not affect children's behavior.
2 There is enough liquid in coffee to counter the chemical that makes you thirsty.
3 Antibiotics are only helpful if the infection is bacterial.

_____
_____
_____
_____
_____
_____
_____
_____
_____
_____

2 Read your partner's paragraphs. Take turns discussing your paragraphs and offer each other advice for improvement.

Applying the principles you have learned in this unit, present your recommendations for assembling and organizing an effective team for a particular business or collaborative group.

PLAN

1 Look back at the work you did in Critical Thinking, page 198, to answer the questions.

1 Which organization will you write your report about?

- ☐ Rockethedge investment bank
- ☐ Saxton, California, professional soccer team
- ☐ Cybergogo, high-tech start-up
- ☐ Smythe University, track program

2 What are the top two or three challenges that the organization faces?

_____

_____

_____

_____

_____

_____

3 If you have chosen an organization that does not yet have a team in place, what are your recommendations for recruitment? If you have chosen an organization that already has members, what are your recommendations for change?

_____

_____

_____

_____

_____

_____

4 What are some recommendations for communication training for your organization?

_____

_____

_____

_____

_____

_____

2 Think about your claim and possible opposing points of view as you answer these questions.

1 What central claim will you make? _____

2 What are other possible points of view? (e.g., *A great team has a lot of high performers on it.*)

_____

_____

_____

3 Why might people believe these are valid points of view?

_____

_____

_____

4 What evidence do you have that supports your own point of view? Highlight possible points in your notes and the readings in this unit, and then summarize your evidence here.

_____

_____

_____

3 Think about the introduction to your report.

- How will you introduce your topic?
- What background information will you provide?
- How will you write your claim to include a concession?

4 Think about your body paragraphs. Each recommendation should have a paragraph and a topic sentence that unites all of the material in that paragraph. Write your ideas here. Then assemble your support for each recommendation.

First body paragraph
Recommendation: _____
Topic sentence: _____
Second body paragraph
Recommendation: _____
Topic sentence: _____
Third body paragraph
Recommendation: _____
Topic sentence: _____

5 Think about your conclusion.

- Refer back to your claim.
- Leave your reader with something to think about.

6 Refer to the Task Checklist on page 203 as you prepare your report.

WRITE A FIRST DRAFT

7 Write your report based on your plan. Write 500–600 words.

REVISE

8 Use the Task Checklist to review your report for content and structure.

TASK CHECKLIST	✔
Have you made a claim?	
Have you acknowledged and countered an alternative point of view?	
Is the audience for your report and the purpose of your report clear to the reader?	
Have you addressed the specific goals and challenges of your organization?	
Have you made recommendations for your organization?	
Have you provided support for your recommendations?	
Does your concluding paragraph refer to your claim and leave your readers something to think about?	

9 Make any necessary changes to your report.

EDIT

10 Use the Language Checklist to edit your report for language errors.

LANGUAGE CHECKLIST	✔
Have you used hedging language in your claim to avoid taking an absolute position?	
Have you used hedged language elsewhere in your report where appropriate?	
Have you followed the standard pattern for concession language, using hedging language where appropriate?	
Have you punctuated your sentences correctly according to the type of hedging and concession you have used?	

11 Make any necessary changes to your report.

ON CAMPUS

THE DYNAMICS OF GROUP WORK

SKILLS

Group projects and activities are a common part of a college education. Group projects are most successful when each person knows their role, understands the tasks, and contributes to the project.

PREPARING TO READ

1 Work with a partner. Discuss the questions.

1 What are the benefits of working on a project as a group?
2 Why are some group projects not successful?
3 Think of a successful group project that you were involved in. What made it successful?

WHILE READING

2 Read the thread from a college discussion board on the next page where students ask for solutions to common problems. Then read the statements below and write *T* (true), *F* (false), or *DNS* (does not say).

_____ 1 The professor should assign several leadership roles in group projects.
_____ 2 There are always some students who prefer not to socialize with people from class.
_____ 3 Successful groups have regular meetings scheduled from the start.
_____ 4 When there is a serious conflict, the group should not involve the professor.
_____ 5 When there is conflict in a group, everyone should take a break to cool off.
_____ 6 Deadlines help people complete their work before the last minute.
_____ 7 People will usually follow the rules of behavior if they have signed a written agreement.

PRACTICE

3 Work with a partner. Imagine you are working on a group project together. Create a list of expectations for your group. Discuss what the group could do if someone is not behaving according to the expectations.

Erin K

I'm wondering if anyone has suggestions for working on a group project. My group is having a lot of problems. What are we doing wrong?

Prof. Bradley

Has your group chosen a team leader? In my classes, that's the first step. That person organizes the meetings and sends out the agenda[1]. For bigger groups or longer projects, there is usually a facilitator who keeps the team on task[2] and a secretary to take notes at meetings.

Burcu O

In my last group, we made a list of expected behaviors: come prepared to all meetings, meet your deadlines, don't talk over other people, ask for help when you need it. It was pretty simple. Then we all signed it. When you sign something, you're more likely to keep your promise.

Juan M

I read that groups should accept the fact that there will be conflict and stress at some point. The best way to deal with it is to discuss it openly when it happens.

Prof. Lester

But sometimes groups have so much conflict they can't work together. If that happens, ask for outside help. In my classes, I want them to come see me or their TA. One of us, or even another student, can act as mediator[3].

Lee C

Erin, another thing is to make sure you schedule all future meetings at your first meeting so everyone can put them on their calendars. Also, set dates for when each draft should be finished. Otherwise everyone will complete their part at the very end.

Erin K

Thank you all for these great ideas. Now I'm really looking forward to my next group project!

---

[1]**agenda** (n) list of discussion topics for a meeting
[2]**on task** (adj phr) working without distraction
[3]**mediator** (n) a person who helps people resolve a disagreement

REAL-WORLD APPLICATION

4 Write a response to Erin with the best advice you have for effective collaboration. Share your ideas in small groups.

GLOSSARY OF KEY VOCABULARY

Words that are part of the Academic Word List are noted with **Ⓐ** in this glossary.

UNIT 1 CONSERVATION

READING 1

capacity Ⓐ (n) ability
deliberate (adj) intentional
emerge Ⓐ (v) to become known
memorabilia (n) a collection of items connected to a person or event
practice (n) a regular or widespread habit or behavior
prompt (v) to cause to do something
recover Ⓐ (v) to get something back
vulnerable (adj) not well protected; able to be harmed

READING 2

affordable (adj) not expensive
deteriorate (v) to grow worse
developers (n) companies that buy land and build on it
facility Ⓐ (n) a building for a special purpose
maintain Ⓐ (v) to continue to claim
prosper (v) to be successful
renovation (n) the repair of a building to bring it into good condition
vacant (adj) empty

UNIT 2 DESIGN

READING 1

appropriate Ⓐ (adj) correct or right for a particular situation
contemporary Ⓐ (adj) existing or happening now
criteria Ⓐ (n pl) standards used for judging something
devoted to Ⓐ (adj) for one particular purpose
donation (n) money or goods given to a person or organization in an attempt to help
human rights (n pl) fair and moral treatment that every person deserves
retain Ⓐ (v) to keep; to continue having
subsequent Ⓐ (adv) next; happening after something else

READING 2

appeal (to) (v) to be interesting or attractive (to)
associate (v) to make a connection in one's mind with
evolve Ⓐ (v) to develop slowly
modify Ⓐ (v) to change somewhat
opposition (to) (n) disagreement with
opt for (v) to choose
resemble (v) to look like
resist (v) to fight against

UNIT 3 PRIVACY

READING 1

abusive (adj) bad and cruel; causing another person mental or physical harm

anonymous (adj) unidentified or unidentifiable

disturbing (adj) upsetting; causing worry

guarantee Ⓐ (v) to promise absolutely and legally

humiliation (n) shame and loss of self-respect

validity Ⓐ (n) reasonableness or acceptability

violate Ⓐ (v) to break, such as a law or agreement

withdraw (v) to stop participating

READING 2

assemble Ⓐ (v) to gather

barrier (n) something that blocks access

eliminate Ⓐ (v) to remove; to get rid of completely

malicious (adj) intentionally hurtful

penalty (n) punishment

prosecute (v) to take to court to determine the guilt of

regulate Ⓐ (v) to control

suspended Ⓐ (adj) not allowed to participate in an activity for a period of time

UNIT 4 BUSINESS

READING 1

aspiring (adj) wishing to become successful

break even (idm) to earn only enough money to pay expenses

component Ⓐ (n) one of the parts of something

fluctuate Ⓐ (v) to change frequently from one level to another

outweigh (v) to be greater or more important than something else

proposition (n) a proposal or suggestion, especially in business

revenue Ⓐ (n) the money that a business receives regularly

transition Ⓐ (n) a change from one state or condition to another

READING 2

accumulate Ⓐ (v) to gradually collect

attainable Ⓐ (adj) able to be reached

follow suit (v phr) to do the same thing

incentive Ⓐ (n) encouragement based on rewards

ongoing Ⓐ (adj) continuing

pioneer (n) one of the first people to do something

retention Ⓐ (n) holding; keeping

shrewdly (adv) based on good judgment

UNIT 5 PSYCHOLOGY

READING 1

intriguing (adj) very interesting; mysterious

label Ⓐ (v) to assign a (usually negative) characteristic to someone or something

norm Ⓐ (n) accepted standard or way of doing something

notion Ⓐ (n) idea

pursue Ⓐ (v) to continue or to try to do something over a period of time

reject Ⓐ (v) to refuse to accept

skeptical (adj) doubting that something is true

suppress (v) to prevent something from being expressed or known

READING 2

breakthrough (n) important discovery that helps solve a problem

confirm Ⓐ (v) to state or show that something is true

innovative Ⓐ (adj) new and different

procrastinator (n) a person who waits as long as possible to begin work

resourceful Ⓐ (adj) skilled at solving problems

seek Ⓐ (v) to try to find or get something

stimulation (n) something that arouses enthusiasm, curiosity, or activity

trigger Ⓐ (v) to cause something to happen or exist

UNIT 6 CAREERS

READING 1

alternative Ⓐ (adj) different from what is usual

assertive (adj) forceful; bold and confident

boast (v) to talk proudly about; to have or own something to be proud of

expertise Ⓐ (n) a high level of knowledge or skill

persistent Ⓐ (adj) strong and determined; lasting for a long time and difficult to resolve

prospective Ⓐ (adj) possible, especially in the future

qualified (adj) having the necessary knowledge or skill

survey Ⓐ (n) a set of questions asked of a large number of people in order to find patterns

READING 2

ambiguity Ⓐ (n) the state of being unclear or having more than one possible meaning

chronic (adj) lasting for a long time, especially something bad

diminish Ⓐ (v) to decrease in size or importance

dispute (v) to disagree with

extend (v) to go further, make bigger, or last longer

founder Ⓐ (n) someone who establishes an organization

illustration Ⓐ (n) an example that explains something

potential Ⓐ (n) the possibility to develop and succeed

UNIT 7 HEALTH SCIENCES

READING 1

bounce back (phr v) to return to normal
counter (v) to oppose; to defend against
cycle (A) (n) repeating series of events
grim (adj) very bad; worrisome
mild (A) (adj) not extreme
revolutionize (A) (v) to completely change
therapeutic (adj) healing; healthful
thrive (v) to live and develop successfully

READING 2

confine (A) (v) to exist in or apply to a limited group or area
detection (A) (n) the notice or discovery of something
domesticated (A) (adj) under human control; used for animals
eradicate (v) to get rid of something completely
facilitate (A) (v) to make something possible or easier
proximity (n) nearness
surge (n) a sudden, large increase
transmission (A) (n) the process of passing something from one person or place to another

UNIT 8 COLLABORATION

READING 1

accomplish (v) to do something successfully
coordinate (A) (v) to make separate things or people work well together
decline (A) (v) to worsen; to decrease
detract from (phr v) to make something worse or less valuable
differentiate (A) (v) to show or find the difference between one thing and another
enhance (A) (v) to improve
isolate (A) (v) to separate something from other connected things
phenomenon (A) (n) something that can be experienced or felt, especially something that is unusual or new

READING 2

apparently (A) (adv) according to what seems to be true
consistent (A) (adj) always behaving or happening in the same way
display (A) (v) to show a feeling or attitude by what you say or do
distraction (n) something that prevents someone from giving full attention to something else
exclusively (A) (adv) only; limited to a specific thing, person, or group
fundamental (A) (adj) basic, being the thing on which other things depend
gesture (n) a movement of the body or a body part to express an idea or feeling
underlie (A) (v) to be the cause of or a strong influence on something

UNIT 1

Reporter: The CD is now a collector's item, replaced by digital downloads. But those who built up music libraries in the 80s and 90s may wonder, how long will those discs work—something Fenella France and her team are hoping to figure out.

Fenella France: You can see this one, it looks pretty good.

Reporter: Right.

France: And then this one.

Reporter: Oh my! France is the chief of preservation research and testing at the Library of Congress.

France: So we've kind of lost the entire reflective layer off of this one.

Reporter: Same CD?

France: Same CD.

Reporter: Produced at the same time.

Reporter: She and her colleagues are studying CDs like this one so they can better understand how to keep them safe for posterity. It turns out not all of the biggest challenges in preserving history involve documents that are centuries old.

One would think, oh, I need to worry about the parchment or the paper degrading, not the things from 20 years ago.

France: That's correct, and that's a challenge, I think. We've always focused on traditional materials, so to speak.

Reporter: How long a CD will last is not as simple as how old it is. Different manufacturers use different methods with vastly different results when it comes to durability.

France: We'd love to be able to say: these particular discs or this specific time, these are the absolute ones at risk. We don't know how people have stored or used them over time, so all of those factors—the use, the handling, the environment—all come into play in terms of the longevity.

Reporter: Which is where the idea of accelerated aging comes in. The CDs are actually cooked in these chambers, and by manipulating the humidity and the temperature, the discs can be aged a certain number of years.

The only thing that's different is how you've artificially aged them?

France: They were aged under the same conditions. One survived, one did not. So that's the challenge we have, that you never quite know how it's going to affect your CD.

Reporter: And if you want to preserve your CD collection at home, here's a few tips.

France: Probably don't put any nice fancy labels onto the top of CDs.

Reporter: And fair warning, you want to avoid those Sharpies.

France: There are some pens that they say don't cause any damage. There's a little piece in the center of the disc, and if you need to, just write on that center region.

Reporter: As for preserving the library's collection, France and her team plan to test the CDs every three to five years to make sure as little as possible is lost to history.

UNIT 2

Man: So, this is what I'm talking about. This is, uh, *Life* magazine, 1953. One ad after another in here—it just kind of shows every single visual bad habit that was, like, endemic in those days. You've got, uh, you know, zany hand lettering everywhere, this swash typography to kind of signify elegance. Exclamation points, exclamation points, exclamation points! Cursive wedding invitation typography down here reading, "Almost everyone appreciates the best." Uh, this was everywhere in the 50s. This is how everything looked in the 50s. You cut to, um—this is after Helvetica was in full swing, same product. No people, no smiling fakery. Just a beautiful, big glass of ice-cold Coke. The slogan underneath: "It's the real thing. Period. Coke. Period." In Helvetica. Period. Any questions? Of course not. Drink Coke. Period. Simple.

Leslie Savan: Governments and corporations love Helvetica because, on one hand, it makes them seem neutral and efficient; but also, it's the smoothness of the letters, makes them seem almost human. That is a quality they all want to convey because, of course, they have the image they're always fighting, that they are authoritarian, they're bureaucratic, you lose yourself in them, they're oppressive. So instead, by using Helvetica, they can come off seeming more accessible, transparent, and accountable.

UNIT 3

Gayle King (co-host): Now to the photo hacking scandal everybody's talking about. As we told you earlier, Apple now says those nude celebrity images were stolen in, quote, "... a very targeted attack on user names, passwords, and security questions ...", adding that "None of the cases we have investigated has resulted from a breach in any of Apple's systems including iCloud® or Find my iPhone." The FBI is now on the case, so we wanted to look at the bigger implications of this. CBS news legal analyst Rikki Klieman joins us from Boston. Rikki, good morning to you.

Rikki Klieman: Good morning.

King: Hey, how is the FBI involved in the case? What exactly are they doing?

Klieman: Well, the FBI is going to look at all of the systems. Despite Apple saying that it really comes from the idea of "forgot your password," they will be looking at the devices belonging to these movie stars—that is, their mobile phones, their computers, their backup systems—and they will also then be searching to look for, in essence, the virtual fingerprints of the hackers themselves.

King: So who do you think could be charged here, the hackers, the websites? The people that posted the videos, the pictures?

Klieman: Well, you have to look from the greatest to the smallest. We know that the hackers can be charged. There's a law on the books as far back as 1986, and it's called the Computer Fraud and Abuse Act. And that's really the big law, because what we have there are penalties for each count, each hacking, and that goes to five years a count and even, with enhancements, it may be more than that. You may remember that there was a case where Scarlett Johansson among others, her nude photos were hacked. The person in Florida who did that, a man by the name of Christopher Chaney, he wound up with a 10-year plea on the basis of nine counts. So he could have gotten a lot more than that. What we look at after that is people who have put it on the website—it's the people who put it up there that may become liable, both criminally and civilly. The website's not going to be liable, and certainly the people who look at it are not going to be liable.

Norah O'Donnell (co-host):   Can I ask you about—there are certainly a lot of headlines out there where people are saying, you know, this isn't just a scandal, it's a sex crime against these women.

Klieman: Well, it's not a sex crime against these women. Uh, the reality of this is, it is a computer crime and a computer crime only, despite the fact that it's this kind of public exposure of something that is really private. When we have something in our cell phone, we have a reasonable expectation of privacy, that no one is going to look at that. But it doesn't mean that by someone hacking into it and putting it out there that it is a sex crime. In fact, the worst part of all of this is—if I read one more thing about people blaming the victims in this case. If you take a photo in the privacy of your own home, with your husband, with your significant other, or all by yourself—and then let alone the fact that some of these photos were deleted—why, in heaven's name, do you expect that some hacker is going to go in there? That is not, it just is not a reasonable expectation of privacy. It is your own, and we shouldn't blame the victim.

Charlie Rose (co-host):   Thank you so much, Rikki.

UNIT 4

Anna Werner (reporter):   Willow Tufano may look like a typical teen, dress like one, and act like one, but growing up during Florida's foreclosure crisis gave her the opportunity to become something else, too.

Willow Tufano: I bought my first house and I'm buying my second house here soon.

Werner: You're a landlord?

Tufano: Yes.

Werner: She's likely Florida's youngest landlord, taking her cues from her realtor mom who buys cheap, bank-owned homes.

Tufano: I would go around with my mom and look at these houses, and there was one that was filled with a whole bunch of furniture that was nice, and I said, well, I could sell this stuff. So that was how it started.

Werner: Willow eventually made $6,000 by selling furniture, which she used to help her purchase this $12,000 home. She'll soon close on her second house, this one. It costs $17,500.

Tufano: I'm trying to get as many houses as I can while the market is low.

Werner: What's your goal?

Tufano: I want to have probably around 10 houses by the time that I'm 18.

Werner: 10?

Tufano: Yes, I want to try for two a year, pretty much.

Werner: Today, Willow spends her spare time gathering and selling items not just from foreclosed homes but from garage sales, from charities, even street curbs.

Tufano: I just try and save every penny that I can to invest in more houses.

Werner: As a minor, Willow can't legally be on the deed. But when she turns 18, her mother, Shannon Moore, will sign the properties over to her.

Shannon Moore: I said, "Willow, lead the way. Show me where you need to go." And she has.

Werner: Not bad for a kid with attention deficit hyperactivity disorder who left a gifted school because teachers told her mom her daughter couldn't focus.

Moore: I guess it's hard to, you know, listen to people say your kid has a problem, you know. And then now look at her. I don't know, I guess I'm really proud of her.

Werner: These days Willow's busy collecting rent from her tenants, shopping for building materials, and taking stock of her next project.

Moore: I think that would work.

Werner: All from a girl who is too young to drive but has plenty of direction. Anna Werner, CBS News, North Port, Florida.

UNIT 5

Charlie Rose (co-host): For 30 years David Kelley and his brother Tom have taken familiar products and made them better. Their design firm IDEO reengineered everything from the computer mouse to television remote controls and even the classroom chair. Now the brothers have put out a new book. It is called *Creative Confidence: Unleashing the Creative Potential within All of Us* [sic]. David and Tom Kelley, welcome.

David and Tom Kelley: Thanks.

Rose: So what is creative confidence?

Tom Kelley: Well, it's really two things. It's the natural human ability to come up with breakthrough ideas combined with the courage to act on those ideas. Because, when we did a hundred interviews for the book, what we discovered is some people have the ideas but they—they have fear of being judged, and so they just hold it all in, and then their idea disappears. And so it's the—it's the ability to come up with the ideas but the courage, too.

Gayle King (co-host): And you both believe that everybody can be creative. I tell you, after looking at the book, I am thinking differently. You said *everybody*. I've never believed that.

David Kelley: Yeah, well, look at little kids in kindergarten.

King: Yes.

David Kelley: Everybody, you know, they're like, they're making like, uh, you know, a picture of a chicken with four legs, and mom puts it up on the refrigerator and says, "Yay!" So, we all have it in kindergarten, and somewhere along the line—

King: In fourth grade, you say.

David Kelley: Yeah, I think it's about fourth grade, you opt out and think of yourself as not creative because you're kind of being judged by your peers, or a teacher tells you that's not a very good drawing, or whatever. And it's just—it's just too bad.

Norah O'Donnell (co-host): I have young children and, you know, I see this happen early on in schools. They say, "Oh, that child is very creative," you know? And you get the assumption that people are born creative, and yet you do not believe that, as Gayle mentioned earlier. But you also think you can teach and continue to foster creativity.

David Kelley: Yeah, I mean, it's funny, you know. Somehow we have, sort of, *creativity* tied up with, kind of, *talent*, and it's really not the case. So, you know, you

don't really expect a person to sit down at the piano and play for the first time. You know, like, that would be crazy. But we somehow think that either you can draw or you can't draw. You know, like, some—drawing takes just as much practice as playing the piano does and so, um, you find your different ways. You may be a creative curator. You may be a creative person who, you know, figures things out in new ways and still can't draw. Right? But, so, creativity is—needs to be defined as the ability to, kind of, come up with new ideas in, kind of, unique ways. If you think about being creative, if you just take all the little parts of a project, what that adds to—and then you say, how can I make this little piece, you know, extraordinary? How can I make this little piece extraordinary?

King: For someone who is listening to you, what is the first thing we should do if we think, I'm not creative.

David Kelley: Yeah.

King: I want to be creative.

David Kelley: Yeah, so, get the book.

King: Other than that.

David Kelley: But the whole thing is—is getting in and building empathy for people. We find that—we see this thing called "bias towards action" where you jump right in. I mean, so many people spend time planning and think, I'm going to go. Instead, just jump in. If you're designing a new, you know, uh, bicycle, go out and watch people ride bicycles. Talk to people who don't ride bicycles. Ride a bicycle yourself. Go to the stores. I mean, all of that, we call it empathy. You're having empathy for the people. If I'm trying to please a certain person, I really want to build empathy for them. And I think it's, kind of, an underserved area. We mostly look at technology or business.

Rose: Yes.

David Kelley: And come up with those kind of ideas and then try to convince people to—that they might like it. It's much better, I believe, to go out and, like, really build empathy for people. What do they really want? What's meaningful to people is really where we go. If it's meaningful for people, then in some ways it's easier to go find technologies and business ideas that solve that particular problem.

UNIT 6

Nick Sinetti: I don't really dig the second shift, but you've got to start somewhere.

Reporter: Despite the worst job market in decades, listen to what 20-year-old Nick Sinetti found right out of high school.

How many offers did you get?

Sinetti: Um, three, I think.

Reporter: Three offers?

Sinetti: Right.

Reporter: He graduated in 2009 as a certified welder from a career in technical education high school, or what used to be called vocational education. He now works for Air Products in Allentown, Pennsylvania. Of the 7,500 employees that you have here in the United States, how many are, what you would say, are the skilled workers?

John McGlade: 4,000.

Reporter: John McGlade is president and CEO of Air Products. His global company designs and builds high-tech hydrogen equipment and devices.
How worried are you that you won't find enough skilled workers in the future?

McGlade: I'm worried. I've been worried.

Reporter: McGlade says he hires about 550 U.S. workers a year—360 are technically skilled positions that require two years of college or advanced certification. These positions can often go unfilled for twelve months.

McGlade: You need people who are electronics experts, who are instrument technicians, who are mechanics that can work on today's modern equipment.

Reporter: But this year funding for vocational education was cut by $140 million, and President Obama is proposing a 20% cut next year.
What is your, sort of, biggest fear if there isn't this continued support for vo-tech education?

McGlade: Without the support and without the continued development of the skilled workforce, um, we're not going to be able to fill the jobs.

Reporter: Lehigh Career and Technical Institute would be impacted as well. Five percent of its budget comes from federal grants.

Teacher: 24 divided by 1.5E, that tells us—

Reporter: The school trains about 3,000 students from across the Lehigh Valley. According to the National Association of Career and Technical schools, these students can earn about $26 an hour more than similar students in non-technical fields.

McGlade: There's going to be more and more of those skilled jobs available that are going to be well paying and be a sustainable career for years and years to come.

Reporter: A career path that McGlade estimates will need 10 million more skilled workers over the next decade.

UNIT 7

Tom Dukes: I never thought it would happen to me.

Katie Couric (reporter): Tom Dukes was the picture of health, an energetic 52-year-old sales executive in Lomita, California, who worked out four hours a day until late last year when he was rushed to the hospital in agonizing pain. An hour later he was on the operating table.

Dukes: I thought, you know, I might just be saying goodbye. That was my last thought.

Couric: Dukes awoke to a shocking reality. Surgeons had to repair a hole in his abdomen caused by a raging E. coli infection developed after eating contaminated meat. This form of E. coli was much more aggressive because it had several genetic mutations making it resistant to antibiotics.

Dukes: Everything was getting, you know, progressively worse quickly.

Couric: Duke's story concerns infectious disease doctors, like Brad Spellberg, author of *Rising Plague*.

Brad Spellberg: These organisms are the experts at resistance.

Couric: He says more infections are starting out as bacteria in food or other ordinary places and evolving into deadly, drug-resistant superbugs.

Spellberg: It is starting to move out of the hospitals and into the communities.

Couric: And what happens to those people?

Spellberg: We're at a point where we may have to start admitting tens of thousands of women with simple urinary tract infections to the hospital.

Couric: Because that infection has outsmarted the pills?

Spellberg: Yep. Because the E. coli that causes most urinary tract infections is becoming resistant.

Couric: Health officials say that resistance is growing, especially among these five deadly bacteria. Virtually all of them carry genes that prevent antibiotics from working, and these genetic mutations are spreading. Another reason for these lethal strains—the overuse of antibiotics. A recent study finds more than 60% of antibiotics prescribed are unnecessary.

John Rex: It's a crisis that touches every country on the globe, touches people of all socioeconomic classes, all races.

Chemist: This represents the compounds that we're making—

Couric: John Rex is the head of drug development for AstraZeneca—one of only a few pharmaceutical companies still devoting resources for new medicines to cure these lethal bugs.

Rex: The trick is to find something that kills the bacteria but doesn't hurt you or me.

Couric: Developing a new antibiotic takes at least ten years and costs as much $1.7 billion. Drug companies make more money creating medicines people take every day for chronic conditions like high blood pressure, insomnia, or sexual dysfunction.
Do you consider this a grave public health crisis?

Spellberg: Yeah. This is a convergence of two public health crises: skyrocketing antibiotic resistance and dying antibiotic development.

Dukes: I was extremely fatigued. I was mentally exhausted.

Couric: It took four months and several drugs for Tom Dukes to finally beat his infection, but he says he'll never completely recover.

Dukes: I think about it every day because if it hadn't worked, I wouldn't be here.

UNIT 8

Carisa Bianci: The company is an advertising agency, but we like to think of ourselves as a creative company. So I think the space was designed to just allow creative thoughts and thinking.

Carol Madonna: Our architect was really smart. He provided us with really indelible materials. We have a thousand 27-year-olds here. They are pretty hard on stuff.

Jayanta Jenkins: The space in itself is designed for collaboration, so I think the mindset just, kind of, you know, very, sort of, fluidly flows that way here.

Jason Clement: I think we really have created this, uh, sense of a city in here where you really have what you need. You know, places where we congregate. We have places where we go away. There are communities, so we're organized by, you know, different projects and different work streams. So, you know, you get a sense of going from, you know, one part of town to another part of town.

Bianci: Main Street is where the creatives are, so all the square boxes there and the three layers of that, that's, kind of, Main Street.

Clement: You can get to the other side of the building by really walking across almost like a catwalk.

Jenkins: The part where we're sitting is a communal space where people can gather to talk about meetings, to go over client reviews, to have lunch.

William Esparza: When it comes to work, it just eliminates the seriousness, you know, and so you can start having ideas and have synergy happen between people informally.

Clement: But you can get work done without having to feel this formality, right, of needing to schedule time or needing to schedule a place to be able to get it done.

Bianci: People can pull over 100 hours a week. Um, it's—it's not uncommon. If you're in a new business pitch, you do a lot of all-nighters. You'll come here on the weekends and there's quite a few cars in the parking lot. You come back the next day, and they're wearing the same outfit that they have. So I think there're spaces here that people can, kind of, crash. Um, there's a whole dog community here.

Clement: Dogs add a lot to a meeting, right, in terms of just humanizing it. I think we can have really tough meetings. We can disagree on things, and if a meeting is particularly tough and somebody starts licking your ankle, it really changes your tone.

Bianci: We tend to do basketball games as well. After hours you're going to see people running up and down that court.

Clement: Everybody shows up and we can get together as a family and share good news and sometimes bad news.

Bianci: I think, you know, whenever someone sees something that they respect and admire, you know, it gives them that, kind of like, all right, you know, I'm going to go and I'm going to, like, take it on, and I want to deliver something as good or better. It's a healthy competitiveness.

Esparza: Whether it's the Gatorade team or the Pepsi team, there's a sense of one-upmanship. You know, you want to make the best work out of the building.

Jenkins: The thing that isn't so nice about an open office plan sometimes is people can always walk in, but if you're really working and don't want to be interrupted, uh, it's nice to find areas in the building where you can see people but they can't see you. You can easily get a lot of work done where people wouldn't be able to find you unless, you know, you decided that you wanted to be found.

Right up above here is this billboard that has one of the Pepsi, um, adverts that we did, and right behind it is the perfect hiding place.

Madonna: We're nurturing everybody and helping them, you know, flourish here, but we also rule with an iron fist.

The authors and publishers acknowledge the following sources of copyright material and are grateful for the permissions granted. While every effort has been made, it has not always been possible to identify the sources of all the material used, or to trace all copyright holders. If any omissions are brought to our notice, we will be happy to include the appropriate acknowledgements on reprinting and in the next update to the digital edition, as applicable.

Text credits

Graphs on pp. 138 and 150 Bureau of Labor Statistics; Graph on p. 140 adapted from Manpower Group "2016/2017 Talent Shortage Survey." Copyright © Manpower Group. Reproduced with kind permission; Graphs on p. 145 adapted from *Education at a Glance 2016: OECD Indicators*, OECD Publishing, Paris. DOI: http://dx.doi.org/10.1787/eag-2016-en. Copyright © 2016 OECD. Reproduced with kind permission; Table on p. 149 Bureau of Labor Statistics; Chart on p. 150 adapted from "U.S. skills gaps." Copyright © Adecco. Reproduced with kind permission; Graph on p. 151 adapted from "The Role of Higher Education in Career Development: Employer Perceptions." Copyright © 2012 The Chronicle of Higher Education. Reproduced with kind permission; Figure on p. 164 adapted from "Clinical Microbiology Reviews: Challenges of Antibacterial Discovery" by Lynn L. Silver. Copyright © 2011 American Society for Microbiology. Reproduced with permission; Graphs on p. 188 adapted from "The Too-Much-Talent Effect: Team Interdependence Determines When More Talent Is Too Much or Not Enough" by Roderick I. Swaab, Michael Schaerer, Eric M. Anicich, Richard Ronay and Adam D. Galinsky. Copyright © SAGE Publications Ltd.

Photo credits

p. 12: Cultura RM Exclusive/Peter Muller/Getty Images; pp. 14–15: pixdeluxe/E+/Getty Images; p. 20: adam smigielski/E+/Getty Images; p. 24: James Pauls/iStock/Getty Images; p. 29: Michael Marquand/Lonely Planet Images/Getty Images; pp. 38–39: Alexander Spatari/Moment/Getty Images; pp. 62–63: Bill Hinton Photography/Moment Open/Getty Images; p. 68: Matthew Horwood/Getty Images News/Getty Images; p. 70: Blackregis/iStock/Getty Images; p. 72: NetPics/Alamy; p. 76: MachineHeadz/E+/Getty Images; pp. 86–87: Jamie Pham Photography/Alamy; p. 90: Jon Hicks/Corbis Documentary/Getty Images; p. 92: Ira Berger/Alamy; p. 93: Jupiterimages/Stockbyte/Getty Images; pp. 110–111: Jeremy Sutton-Hibbert/Getty Images News/Getty Images; pp. 116 and 124: Imagno/Hulton Archive/Getty Images; p. 121: Michael Ochs Archives/Getty Images; pp. 134–135: Boston Globe/Getty Images; pp. 158–159: Tim Graham/Getty Images News/Getty Images; pp. 182–183: Brian Babineau/National Basketball Association/Getty Images; p. 190: Ababsolutum/E+/Getty Images; p. 194 (photo a): lisa kimberly/Moment/Getty Images; p. 194 (photo b): LuminaStock/Vetta/Getty Images; p. 194 (photo c): Cary Wolinsky/Aurora/Getty Images; p. 194 (photo d): Darren Robb/Taxi/Getty Images.

Front cover photographs by (man) Dean Drobot/Shutterstock and (background) vichie81/Shutterstock.

Illustrations

Oxford Designers & Illustrators pp. 46, 118, 131.

We are grateful to the following companies for permission to use copyright logos:

p. 43: IKEA; p. 44: FedEx, World Wildlife Fund, Human Rights; p. 48; NBC, BP, Spotify; p. 49: Tropicana.

Video Supplied by BBC Worldwide Learning.

Video Stills Supplied by BBC Worldwide Learning.

Corpus

Development of this publication has made use of the Cambridge English Corpus (CEC). The CEC is a multi-billion word computer database of contemporary spoken and written English. It includes British English, American English, and other varieties of English. It also includes the Cambridge Learner Corpus, developed in collaboration with the University of Cambridge ESOL Examinations. Cambridge University Press has built up the CEC to provide evidence about language use that helps to produce better language teaching materials.

Cambridge Dictionaries

Cambridge dictionaries are the world's most widely used dictionaries for learners of English. The dictionaries are available in print and online at dictionary.cambridge.org. Copyright © Cambridge University Press, reproduced with permission.

URLS

The publisher has made every effort to ensure that the URLs for external websites referred to in this book are correct and active at the time of printing. However, the publisher takes no responsibility for the websites and can make no guarantees that sites will remain live or that their content is or will remain appropriate.

Typeset by emc design ltd

INFORMED BY TEACHERS

Classroom teachers shaped everything about *Prism*. The topics. The exercises. The critical thinking skills. The On Campus sections. Everything. We are confident that *Prism* will help your students succeed in college because teachers just like you helped guide the creation of this series.

Prism Advisory Panel

The members of the *Prism* Advisory Panel provided inspiration, ideas, and feedback on many aspects of the series. *Prism* is stronger because of their contributions.

Gloria Munson
University of Texas, Arlington

Kim Oliver
Austin Community College

Gregory Wayne
Portland State University

Julaine Rosner
Mission College

Dinorah Sapp
University of Mississippi

Christine Hagan
George Brown College/Seneca College

Heidi Lieb
Bergen Community College

Stephanie Kasuboski
Cuyahoga Community College

Global Input

Teachers from more than 500 institutions all over the world provided valuable input through:
- Surveys
- Focus Groups
- Reviews